Peter Guthrie Tait, Balfour Stewart

Paradoxical Philosophy

A Sequel to the Unseen Universe

Peter Guthrie Tait, Balfour Stewart

Paradoxical Philosophy
A Sequel to the Unseen Universe

ISBN/EAN: 9783337076221

Printed in Europe, USA, Canada, Australia, Japan

Cover: Foto ©Thomas Meinert / pixelio.de

More available books at **www.hansebooks.com**

Seventh Edition, Revised and Enlarged.

THE UNSEEN UNIVERSE;

OR

Physical Speculations on a Future State.

BY

BALFOUR STEWART AND P. G. TAIT.

Crown 8vo. 6s.

MACMILLAN AND CO., LONDON.

PARADOXICAL PHILOSOPHY.

> From floating elements in chaos hurl'd,
> Self-form'd of atoms, sprang the infant world.
> No great *First Cause* inspired the happy plot,
> But all was matter, and no matter what.
> Atoms, attracted by some law occult,
> Settling in spheres, the globe was the result;
> Pure child of *Chance*, which still directs the ball,
> As rotatory atoms rise or fall.
>
> I sing how casual bricks in airy climb
> Encountered casual horse-hair, casual lime,
> How rafters, borne through wondering clouds elate,
> Kissed in their slope blue elemental slate.
>
> Oh! happy age when convert Christians read
> No sacred writings but the Pagan creed,
> Oh! happy age when, spurning Newton's dreams,
> Our poets' sons recite Lucretian themes,
> Abjure the idle systems of their youth,
> And turn again to atoms and to truth!—HORACE SMITH.

Yesterday, when weary with writing, and my mind quite dusty with considering these atoms, I was called to supper, and a salad I had asked for was set before me. 'It seems then,' said I aloud, 'that if pewter dishes, leaves of lettuce, grains of salt, drops of water, vinegar and oil, and slices of eggs, had been floating about in the air from all eternity, it might at last happen by chance that there would come a salad.' 'Yes,' says my wife, 'but *not so nice and well-dressed as this of mine is.*'—KEPLER.

PARADOXICAL PHILOSOPHY

A SEQUEL TO

THE UNSEEN UNIVERSE

In te, Domine, speravi, non confundar in æternum.

SECOND EDITION

London
MACMILLAN AND CO.
MDCCCLXXIX.

EGO SVM RESVRRECTIO ET VITA
QVI CREDIT IN ME ETIAM SI MORTVVS FVERIT
VIVET.

'Almighty God, give us grace that we may cast away the works o[f] darkness, and put upon us the armour of light, now in the time of thi[s] mortal life, in which thy Son Jesus Christ came to visit us in great humility[,] that in the last day, when he shall come again in his glorious Majesty t[o] judge both the quick and dead, *we may rise to the life immortal*, throug[h] him who liveth and reigneth with thee and the Holy Ghost, now and ever[.] *Amen.*'

TO

THE PRESENT AND FORMER PRESIDENTS

AND THE OTHER MEMBERS

OF THE

PARADOXICAL,

THIS BRIEF ACCOUNT OF THE SOCIETY'S JUBILEE MEETING

IS DEDICATED BY

THE EDITORS.

PREFACE.

A WORD or two may perhaps be necessary as to the form in which this book is cast.

The exigencies of the subject, and not any thought of imitating Peacock, Helps, or Mallock—far less Christopher North, Bunyan, or Plato—absolutely *dictated* the conversational style.

The Paradoxical Society is a real and living power, well known far beyond its membership; and the Editors have to record with gratitude the assistance rendered to them by various members of that body in the compilation of this little volume.

October, 1878.

CONTENTS.

CHAPTER I.
THE PARADOXICAL SOCIETY, ... PAGE 1

CHAPTER II.
CHOOSING THE SUBJECT, . . . 17

CHAPTER III.
DR. STOFFKRAFT OPENS THE DEBATE, . . 55

CHAPTER IV.
THE REPLY, ... 85

CHAPTER V.
THE CONFERENCE IN THE YEW TREE AVENUE, . 123

CHAPTER VI.
CONCLUSION OF THE DEBATE, . . . 142

CHAPTER VII.
WHAT BECAME OF THE DOCTOR, . 203

CHAPTER I.

THE PARADOXICAL SOCIETY.

'All concord 's born of contraries.'
BEN JONSON, *Cynthia's Revels.*

AT the time when our tale commences the Paradoxical Society had almost arrived at the mature age of fifty years, having been brought into being in 1826 by the well-known Isaac Fairbank.

On so solemn an occasion the time-honoured custom of celebrating by a feast multiples and sub-multiples of centuries of life could not of course be omitted.

The founder of the society had long since been gathered to his fathers, but his only son Stephen was allowed on all sides to be no unworthy descendant of that sagacious old lover of truth and fair play.

Stephen had in his youth achieved distinction in one of our great English Universities, and as a logical consequence he was not disposed to pass the remainder of his life without taking an active part in the work of the world.

Indeed his father Isaac had always looked to his son to maintain the credit of a large industrial concern which would naturally revert to him as a species of patrimony.

What now was Stephen to do with this inheritance? Sell its fixtures and good-will, buy acres and hunt? Such a course did not recommend itself to the son, nor indeed would his father have readily suffered its adoption. 'If Stephen inherits my means he also inherits my duties,' the old man was heard to say; and so after his university career, this worthy son of a true *alma mater*, nothing loth, settled himself down in his father's counting-house, and buckled on his commercial armour just before business hours.

Such filial piety did not remain unrewarded, and the son's hours of leisure were soon solaced by the distinguished privilege of admission into the Paradoxical Society, which met regularly once a month under the presidency of his father.

Stephen was most praiseworthy in his attendance at all these meetings—first as a listener only—afterwards as a speaker also.

Here he would sit for hours enchanted by the pleasant flow of varied and good-natured discussion, touching upon everything and yet wounding no one.

Nothing was too great, nothing too small, for these easy but not thoughtless philosophers. They went over the whole house of knowledge from attic to basement, preceded by their President, lantern in hand like a second Diogenes; they entered every room, they threw the rays into every corner, they ransacked every cupboard, they tapped every wall.

Meanwhile the well-arranged collections, conveniently displayed in cabinets, received but little attention; indeed the old man had an original and very simple theory on the subject of these collections.

He imagined that in addition to its more prominent furniture each room had its individual *bête noire*, its skeleton in the cupboard, its little private weakness concealed from the inquirer as sedulously as its strong points were ostentatiously displayed before him, and the search of the President was invariably after these weaknesses, many of which he succeeded in discovering during the course of a long and persevering life. Need we add that whenever he met with a triumph of this kind the trophy was exhibited and discussed at the next meeting of the Paradoxical.

But we must not imagine from all this that the old man was a disbeliever in human honesty and truth; on the contrary, he was in reality one of the most patient and humble seekers for these two good things this world has ever seen.

Nor must we imagine that he was altogether a cynic—far from it; he had doubtless a shrewd eye for the weakness of his adversary, and a quick wit to take advantage of it—a combination which rendered him really dangerous.

Time however will overcome the best of us, and at length this genial but yet terrible old man was gathered to his fathers.

In due course the son was unanimously chosen as President of the Paradoxical, and it was then seen that he was in some respects even better qualified than his father for the duties of such a post.

He had not perhaps his father's genius, nor was he able to detect at a glance the weak points in his adversaries' harness. He was not a collector of weaknesses, but on the other hand he inherited and studied profoundly the large mass of such materials which his father had gathered together, and thus through a kind of comparative anatomy he at length attained a very comprehensive knowledge of the various schools of thought. But along with their weakness he studied also their strength, and a combined use of both gave him ultimately a rare grasp of the subject before him.

The father was like the detective who brings into court a list of the delinquencies of the culprit, but the son was the judge who, when he has listened to both sides of the question, sums up the evidence convincingly for the benefit of the jury.

Such, in the year 1876, was the owner of Elmsly House, an old-fashioned residence formerly belonging to a family now extinct. But the ancient genius of the place still lingered about it, not having suffered violent treatment at the hands of the present proprietor at the time when he adapted the house to the requirements of his family and of modern civilisation. The old garden especially, with its broad green walks, and the mile-long yew-tree avenue, were relics of the past, fondly cherished by their present owner.

Placed in a region of great natural beauty, the usual course with an Englishman would have been to circle his domain round with a wall as high as he could afford to make it, on the same principle that the good-wife of Broeck cleans her parlour window to let the sun in, and then closes the shutter to keep it out.

But Stephen Fairbank was an exception to this rule. An ardent lover of nature, he had opened up many delightful outlooks into the beautiful distance from various parts of his grounds. In this pleasant place, on the eve of Whitsuntide 1876, great preparations were being made for the approaching jubilee. The members of the club had agreed in selecting this time as the very best opportunity for its celebration, for it was thought that they had a better chance of bringing men together from various quarters during this short holiday than in the long vacation, which each man is disposed to utilise after a fashion of his own.

Add to this, that if the weather should prove favourable, a good deal of the discussion might be conducted in the open air, and by moving about from place to place they might even convert themselves into a school of peripatetic philosophers.

The most important member of the home circle was Frederick Fairbank, the host's eldest son, a young and rising barrister who had distinguished himself at Cambridge even more than his father had done thirty years before. He was a striking instance of that strange law by which family peculiarities, in descending, frequently leap over one generation with the view apparently of acquiring sufficient impetus to fasten them with redoubled pertinacity upon the next. A general objector to every conclusion that was not absolutely sure from its very foundation, he was not, however, by any means a Mephistopheles, nor did he range himself, either from choice or profession, invariably against the side of goodness and virtue. To him the side which he took was apparently a matter of indifference, if only he might get the chance of dealing an unexpected blow.

He was like a military engineer who first sets himself to construct an armour-plate sufficiently strong to resist all known projectiles, and, after succeeding, constructs a gun sufficiently powerful to pierce the plate.

Always keeping his own counsel, no one knew where to have him in any dispute; while he, on the contrary, had a perfect knowledge of the weak points of both parties.

We must next make our readers acquainted with the Rev. Ralph Bemerton, B.D., vicar of the parish in which Stephen Fairbank lived. Permitting neither his piety to interfere with his general cultivation, nor his general cultivation with his piety, he nevertheless considered the duties of his parish to form his chief work. He was a lover of antiquity, and held fast by Catholic tradition, separating however between that which was manifestly a product of time and that which he considered to be essential. He was likewise a diligent, and in some respects a successful, student of physical and natural science, the true characteristics of which he would not for a moment admit to be incompatible with those of religion.

It was even rumoured that he had dabbled somewhat in the Divine art, and that should the recesses of his desk ever be examined they would be found to contain a poem celebrating the past glories of the old family, now extinct, to whom the surrounding district had, generations ago, belonged.

When pressed upon this subject he was understood to admit the soft impeachment, alleging at the same time the engrossing claims of his parish duties as an excuse for the non-completion of his literary work.

Our catalogue would be incomplete if we forgot the distinguished East Indian, Sir Kenneth M'Kelpie, K.S.I., who was one of the guests on the present occasion. A Scot of Scots, he had very much of the shrewdness of his countrymen, with perhaps a tinge of some of their peculiarities.

As an instance of the former we may remark that in early life he had been content to forsake the barren glories of his hereditary moor for more profitable if less exalted pastures in the East.

As an instance of the latter, Sir Kenneth, if he did not believe in second-sight, and its long train of affiliated mysteries, was yet disposed to represent the subject as one which, in his own opinion, and in that of all unprejudiced persons, must be regarded as open for discussion.

Owing to his high culture and formidable originality, he had a way of putting things which had already secured him many adherents. We remember his quaint account of the first séance at which he had been present. 'I asked the medium,' he said, 'when and where my father had died? and it was not till a year afterwards that I discovered he had made a mistake.' Knowing the gentle yet insidious mysticism of his guest, the wily host had endeavoured to balance it on this occasion by the vigorous oratory of Elijah Holdfast, Member of Parliament for one of the Northern Counties, well known and not unfrequently listened to in the House of Commons. This rising statesman was not to be taken in, and it was a matter of great interest and much speculation amongst the guests whether the quaint and exquisitely subtle suggestions of Sir Kenneth would finally prevail, or would be forced to yield to the sledge-hammer oratory of this modern Boanerges.

But the most distinct personality among the guests invited by Stephen Fairbank on this occasion was undoubtedly Dr. Hermann Stoffkraft, the well-known German Philosopher.

Picture to yourself a little man, enthusiastic, single-hearted, sincere, and withal perfectly amiable, with a sanguine complexion, and with prominent eyes generally seen behind spectacles, active in his habits, and always rushing about, and you have a very fair notion of the outward man.

With regard to his mental characteristics, they were not like those of ordinary mortals. In this country we should probably (in the rough way we have of lumping men together) call him a materialist, but Dr. Hermann Stoffkraft might no doubt be inclined to contest the propriety of the name. He called himself a votary of the goddess Nature, apparently using that word to denote not merely the orderly succession of external phenomena with which we are brought into contact, but likewise the Power which underlies these manifestations.

But he was by no means a blind worshipper, in fact he was compelled reluctantly to admit that in one little matter his goddess had made a mistake.

This mistake consisted, according to him, in the development of a race of intelligent beings like ourselves.

This was the only blot on her escutcheon—the rift within the lute—the one incongruous feature that marred her otherwise perfect beauty.

He had often and anxiously pondered over this little point, at first in the hope that it might be found to denote a strictly local outbreak, just as every good man is bound to hope that an epidemic may be confined to one locality, but a more profound study had brought home to his reluctant mind the conviction that the disease was probably as extensive as the universe itself.

As he had no enemies, the task of criticising these utterances of the little Doctor of course fell to his friends, from whom we have derived this description, and who used now and then to hint that the Doctor would have preferred a universe presided over by his favourite goddess, with only Hermann Stoffkraft to sing her praises.

As, however, he had not been consulted on this point, and as numerous candidates for the office of chief singer had already appeared, especially in his native country, these would-be critics were understood to imply that the Doctor had been rather piqued, and had in consequence retaliated by proposing to regard the whole system as a mistake.

Be this as it may, he had evidently persuaded himself that he was right, and his transparent sincerity and consistency of conduct could not be disputed, although perhaps the more sagacious of his friends understood the Doctor well enough to doubt that he would always remain faithful to his present creed.

These were the more prominent members of the company assembled at Elmsly House on the Saturday evening preceding Whitsunday.

Our readers may perhaps be interested in the following conversation which then took place:

Stephen Fairbank.—I propose, gentlemen, that to-morrow morning such of you as please should go with me to hear our friend Bemerton preach, for I rather think he will give us a very good discourse. I am not sure, however, whether Dr. Stoffkraft will care to go, as he probably entertains peculiar opinions upon the subject of church-going.

Dr. Hermann Stoffkraft.—My dear Sir, I shall be glad to go. I am a student of human nature, and hope to derive much instruction from being present, even if I do not echo the sentiments of the preacher. But (*here the little Doctor put on an arch expression*) I hope you will not press me to sign anything.

All.—Sign anything! why, Doctor, what makes you think of such a thing?

Dr. Hermann Stoffkraft.—Because I have just parted from my distinguished American friend Lucretius O. Blazeforth, who tells me that the last time he went to church he had to sign something.

The Rev. Ralph Bemerton (laughing).—When a similar occasion arises in the history of Dr. Stoffkraft I need not say that my church will be very much at his service.

Stephen Fairbank (laughing also).—And I, for my part, will place my house, with equal good-will, at the Doctor's service, and perhaps if he stays here long enough I may be able to afford him an opportunity of finding the prime requisite.

Dr. Hermann Stoffkraft.—Many thanks, my dear friends, but that will never be; you know my opinions.

Stephen Fairbank.—Perhaps these may change, Doctor. Sensible people are not wedded for ever to the same opinions.

After this conversation the Doctor was in more than usual good humour for the rest of the evening.

CHAPTER II.

CHOOSING THE SUBJECT.

'Much upon this riddle runs
The wisdom of the world.'
SHAKSPERE, *Measure for Measure.*

ON Sunday after service (which the Doctor attended in full evening dress), the weather being fine, a walk was proposed in the direction of the ruins, and the party started off, fully prepared to utilise the occasion for at least a preliminary discussion. Sir Kenneth was the first to speak.

Sir Kenneth M'Kelpie.—Something in the service to-day brought to my mind the two ways of viewing the universe—the idealistic and the materialistic.

The idealist generally asserts that the laws of the universe mean only the mode in which the Supreme Being trammels finite intelligences with regard to time, space, and sensation. He thus starts with himself—a conditioned being, and with a Supreme Power underlying all phenomena and influencing all finite intelligences after an orderly manner. On the other hand, the materialist, failing to grasp the underlying Power, attaches a reality to external phenomena which the idealist will not admit.

Now, I am not at present going to argue the point at issue between the two schools, nor will I dilate upon the distinction which metaphysicians make between *noumena* and *phenomena*, but I should wish nevertheless to point out that in my opinion the theological doctrine that would confine the term *substance* or *essence* to that Power which underlies phenomena is by no means inconsistent with our appretiation of the practical reality of external things.

It has been recently said[1] that our 'practical working certainty of the reality of matter depends upon the facts, *firstly*, that it offers

---

[1] *Unseen Universe*, page 103.

resistance to our imagination and our will, and, *secondly*, that in particular it offers *absolute* resistance to all attempts to change its quantity.'

Frederick Fairbank.—While agreeing generally with what has just been said, I yet object to the manner in which Sir Kenneth has brought together the three words time, space, and sensation, as if each were independent of the others. I think I can conceive of a being with no impression of space, while I feel sure I cannot conceive of a being without some impression of time. I can, for instance, conceive a man in good health to be so comfortably placed—let us say in bed, in the dark, that virtually he is not brought into contact with any external reality. He is not even conscious of having a body, because he experiences no such inequality of sensation as might recall this circumstance to his mind. On the other hand, not being engrossed with any fatiguing train of thought, he is equally unconscious of having a head and brain. And yet the very circumstance of his conscious existence and enjoyment gives him the impression of time, while from the placid nature of his external surroundings he fails to attain the impression of space.

Sir Kenneth M‘Kelpie.—There is I fancy a good deal of truth in this distinction, and we must allow that it is impossible for a conscious being wholly to get rid of the idea of time. Indeed, I suppose that when your friend has attained perfect equality of sensation he will at once fall asleep—the very act of sensation implying inequality.

Stephen Fairbank.—I am unwilling to interrupt this pleasant discussion, but I cannot help being amused at the haste with which you have both branched off into a side issue, while here is our friend Stoffkraft ready, and even anxious, to give us his views on the main subject.

Dr. Hermann Stoffkraft.—I for my part am willing to allow that something analogous to the idealistic mode of viewing the universe best represents the truth. To my mind the Cosmos without an underlying power is a structure without a backbone—it is a thing which cannot withstand the vigorous blows of a thoroughly sound and common sense philosophy, but must ultimately collapse. I say ultimately, because like a gigantic octopus such a theory may throw out numerous arms in various directions, and grapple with its adversaries in a very unpleasant manner, but it cannot ultimately prevail. Such a creature, if only big enough, could seize its prey long after its body had been smashed to pieces. Indeed, thinkers who differ in everything else appear to agree on this point. Hume, for instance, acknowledges it. 'The whole frame of nature,' he tells us in his Natural History of Religion, 'bespeaks an intelligent author; and no rational inquirer can, after serious reflection, suspend his belief a moment with regard to the primary principles of genuine Theism and religion.'

I presume that we all agree about this necessity, although we very probably differ as to how far we are entitled to attribute a certain character to the Author of the universe.

This, it seems to me, is the real point in dispute, and it is well known that Hume 'professed himself unable to reconcile the facts of the world with Infinite Power and Goodness, and therefore disposed on his own part to allow a more moderate conception of a God.'[1]

I confess that in this respect I agree with Hume, but I must not wander from the present subject. I will therefore return to the evidence we have for an intelligent designer of the universe.

Now, in the first place, I cannot see that this evidence can possibly be upset by any theory with regard to the method in which these designs have been carried out—that it can, for instance, be upset by the theory of Evolution I utterly deny.

Before the advent of this theory it was usual for those who followed a certain class of theologians to imagine that our first parents sprang in a moment, ready-made, into the

---

[1] See the article in the *Quarterly Review* for 1869, entitled 'The Argument of Design.'

possession of a mature physical and moral nature. Now why this view should be held to be more in accordance with religion, nay, why it should be held to be more in accordance with the Bible, than the hypothesis of evolution I cannot comprehend.[1] We all of us acknowledge that in the case of the individual our whole nature, physical, intellectual, and moral, has been developed from what we may term an insignificant beginning—why should we therefore set ourselves against the hypothesis which presumes that a similar course of procedure may have been adopted in the history of our race?

The Rev. Ralph Bemerton.—It is not, I imagine, the theory of Evolution to which theologians object. Indeed, if we view the word as expressive of orderly development, evolution becomes at once a theological doctrine. It is rather the abuse of this theory by mechanical bigots that is repulsive to the theologian. Certain of the philosophers, not of the genuine men of

---

[1] 'Adam, which was the son of God.'—Luke iii. 38.

science, seem to be forming themselves into a caste, with a dogma of their own, and to be developing into as fine specimens of the genus bigot as the Inquisition ever encouraged. For instance, we know that one class of writers challenges the verdict of design on account of certain enigmatical parts of Nature. These cite with this view the existence of rudimentary organs in man, and ask what useful purpose such organs can be meant to serve. To my mind traces like these are no less valuable than the occurrence of fossils in geological strata, for they indicate to us the way in which the great Designer has been pleased to work. Indeed, these rudimentary organs and other relics of the past appear, when viewed in this light, to furnish the crowning proof of design, because they would seem to imply a provision for the intellectual adolescence of our race, just as a wise parent opens his mind and method of working to the son who is arriving at a mature age.

Sir Kenneth M'Kelpie.—There is, however, another objection to the argument for design to which no allusion has yet been made. I mean that derived from the infinite nature of God.

What right have we, it may be said, to attribute design to an eternal and all-powerful Being? Is design not rather a word expressive of the mode by which our own finite intelligences work, than one which denotes the mode of operation of the Divine Mind? To all this I would reply, in the first place, by asking whether it be not a mere quibble on the difference (such as it is) between *design* and *purpose?* and next, by the remark that, if we contemplate the Deity at all (and I hold that we are bound to do so as far as we can), we must develop from the platform on which we have been placed, and it is surely unnecessary to say that we must develop upwards instead of downwards. Perhaps, after all, my friend Frederick was right when he told us that the notion of time forces itself on us in a way that that of space does not, and that we can more easily conceive of a Being existing without reference to space than of one existing without reference to time. Let us therefore take this last and most essential condition, and see what we reach by developing upwards. In the first place, I can conceive of a Being whose rapidity and capacity of thought in the present are immeasurably greater than those of man. In the next place, I can conceive of a Being whose memory of past events is immeasurably more vivid than that of man, so that the past is virtually always present before Him. Thirdly, I can conceive of a Being whose prevision of the future is immeasurably greater than that of man, so that the future is likewise virtually present before Him. Fourthly, I can conceive of a Being whose existence goes immeasurably far back, and will go immeasurably far forward. Fifthly and lastly, I can imagine such a Being embracing all space, so that nothing is external to Him. In fine, it appears to me that I can only approach the mysterious Imposer of conditions by bringing before me an infinite conditioned Being. No doubt this method is imperfect, but I can do no more. I must accept the conditions imposed upon me, and think by means of time and space, although I well know that these are not trammels to the Divine Being in the same sense as they are to me. For, with regard to the Deity, they form conditions which He imposes on His creation, while, with regard to myself, they represent the conditions which the Creator imposes upon me.

Dr. Hermann Stoffkraft.—I may say that I quite agree with nearly every word which Sir Kenneth has spoken.

We must regard the relation of the Deity to space and time very much as Sir Kenneth says. I think, too, that we must regard Him as very wise and very powerful. I will not say infinitely wise or infinitely powerful, because it is impossible that we should attain to any kind of proof of infinite wisdom or infinite power— eternal power I grant, but not infinite power.

So much I make out from a contemplation of the Universe, but I do not from the same source perceive that He is absolutely good. Perhaps I am not justified in saying that

He is not so, but I think I am justified in asserting that if His goodness be perfect, then His power and wisdom are not infinite; or, on the other hand, that if His power and wisdom be infinite, then His goodness is not perfect. In saying so, I am, of course, aware that I am using the terms power, wisdom, and goodness in a human sense, and I freely concede to my opponents whatever advantage they may think they derive from the concession.

These are the conclusions to which I have been brought by considering the universe in which I dwell.

Sir Kenneth M'Kelpie.—I am not now going to contest these conclusions, but I should like to bring before the learned Doctor a somewhat curious point. I daresay he will think me a mystic, but I maintain that mysticism is an inherent element in the discussion of such problems as those now before us.

What I wish to point out is that, in certain geometrical and physical problems, infinity comes to us in two ways. Let us, first of all, take the case (quoted by Professor Jevons) of a horizontal fixed straight line which we may imagine to be indefinitely extended in both directions; next let there be another straight line, also indefinitely extended, moveable round some point above the fixed line, and cutting that line towards the right. If, now, this line be made to revolve with a rotation, the opposite to that of the hands of a watch, the point at which it cuts the fixed line will move to the right, and when both lines have become parallel, this point will have moved to an infinite distance in that direction. But mark what will happen if the rotation be continued beyond this limit: the point of intersection having already marched off to an infinite distance on the right, will now appear at and return from an infinite distance on the left. Thus a progress *towards infinity* in the one direction is supplemented by a progress *from infinity* in the other.

Something of a very similar kind occurs in optics :—

Suppose, for instance, that we have a concave mirror, and let us begin by placing a luminous object at its centre, then its image will be at the centre likewise. Now let the luminous object move gradually from the centre to the principal focus; while this goes on its image will move rapidly outwards from the centre to infinity, say, on the left. Continue the progress of the luminous object from the principal focus towards the mirror, and mark what will then take place. The image which had proceeded to infinity on the left will at once make its appearance at an infinite distance on the right, and rapidly approach the mirror, so that, when the object shall have reached the mirror, its image will be there likewise. Here, too, a progress towards infinity in the one direction is supplemented by a progress from infinity in the other. In fine, it appears to me that wherever any sort of progress towards infinity is conceivable, such, to be complete as a hypothesis, requires to be supplemented by a corresponding progress from infinity in the opposite direction. If, therefore, the development of the individual onwards and upwards into the eternity of the future be a conceivable hypothesis, it requires, I feel sure, to be supplemented by a corresponding development downwards from the eternity of the past; and more especially if immortality be a truth, and if we are to have relations onwards and upwards with a spiritual unseen throughout a future eternity, I should expect that these would necessarily presuppose relations with a spiritual unseen bearing down upon us from a past eternity.

I think that if we ponder on these views they will be found to contain a plea for the necessity of revelation, and will be found likewise to combat the objection to the possibility of immortality derived from the fact that we have a beginning, and must therefore expect to have an end. I speak, however, as a mystic.

The Rev. Ralph Bemerton.—While a study of the works of Nature must, I think, lead every one up to some conception of God, yet this conception must, it is clear, be necessarily imperfect. For what do we do?[1] 'We start with a

---

[1] See *Unseen Universe*, page 18.

single intellectual being who is applying himself to a scientific study of the works of Nature. The idea of our neighbour does not enter into it, and we agree to regard ourselves as intellectual rather than as moral or social beings. The result is that, having voluntarily confined our argument to one channel, we obtain a knowledge of God's character, which is necessarily incomplete.' I quite agree with what Sir Kenneth has said about there being two ways through which we are brought into contact with the infinite, although the infinity of which he gave us examples is, properly speaking, the reciprocal of a conceivable quantity varying continuously through zero. I am not quite sure, however, that I hold the distinction between natural and revealed religion to be so marked as he seems inclined to make it. I feel rather disposed to look upon man as being in a state of childhood, or let us say early youth, and upon God as acting towards him like a wise father, leaving him to develop his own faculties by his own use of them, but at the same time continually watching over him and wisely interfering when necessary, always, however, in such a manner as not to put his intellect to permanent confusion.

It seems to me that, in order to render complete the argument derived from Nature, it must be made to embrace with the external universe a study of man himself, that we must therefore take account of history, and specially that great and complicated historical problem—the rise and progress of Christianity. Here, then, we are at once brought into contact with revelation. I confess I think that the only result of drawing a hard and fast line between the natural and the revealed has been to divide us into two separate and seemingly hostile camps, the one under the banner of science and the other under that of religion.

Dr. Hermann Stoffkraft.—To return for a moment to what Sir Kenneth has said, I would ask if his doctrine does not in some sense involve that of a past eternity of the universe, or, in other words, of a past eternity of matter?

I have always understood that this is a doctrine eminently repugnant to theologians as such.

The Rev. Ralph Bemerton.—The doctrine of the past eternity of the universe implies, no doubt, the past eternity of the conditioned, but does it therefore imply that the matter or stuff which we now behold has existed from all eternity? I certainly fail to perceive that the one doctrine necessarily implies the other.

By this time the party had reached the ruins, through which the Rev. Ralph Bemerton undertook to be their guide, while he gave them an account of the family now extinct, who had long ago been lords of the district.

The Rev. Ralph Bemerton.—The St. Claudes were an old Norman family, who, having settled in this country, seem speedily to have secured the attachment of their dependents; they became, in fact, a recognised race of hereditary chieftains.

Ruling well and lovingly, one would have expected that their days would be long in the land. But where are they now? Their name and race have utterly disappeared. There is no evidence to show that they were violent partizans of either of the two great rival Plantagenet houses which contested the throne, but they fell before an enemy not less dreadful than the demon of civil war.

As he spoke the party entered the ruined chapel, which contained the graves of the family, and their attention was attracted to one corner in which there were a number of monuments apart by themselves—

> 'Each bearing the form of a maiden fair
> With her hands clasped meekly, as if in prayer,
> And a saint-like calm on her pallid face:
> The calm of the just who has run his race. . . .'[1]

One of these monuments bore the following inscription :—

ELIZABETH St. CLAUDE,

OB. JUN. 15, 1475, AET. XVII.

OMNIS CARO FENUM, ET OMNIS GRATIA EIUS QUASI FLOS AGRI. EXSICCATUM EST FENUM ET CECIDIT FLOS QUIA SPIRITUS DOMINI SUFFLAVIT IN EO ;—VERE FENUM EST POPULUS :— EXSICCATUM EST FENUM ET CECIDIT FLOS ; VERBUM AUTEM DOMINI MANET IN ETERNUM.

Dr. Hermann Stoffkraft was the first to break the silence imposed by the solemnity of the surroundings. 'Well,' he said, 'I suppose

---

[1] From the unpublished MS. of the Rev. Ralph Bemerton, B.D.

that with families as with individuals very often the best die soon. It requires a tough nature to stand long. Life brings little but suffering, and death can thus be no real loss.'

The party soon began to turn homewards, and Stephen Fairbank ventured to remind them that one-half only of the original subject of conversation had yet been discussed. The idealistic theory of the universe, he told them, assumed the existence of the individual, and he should like much to know what they thought about this assumption.

Dr. Hermann Stoffkraft.—The existence of the individual follows logically from the conclusions upon which we are all agreed.

We are all of us advocates of a hypothesis more or less idealistic : now such a hypothesis appears to me to imply the specific distinction of the individual.

A practical conviction of the reality of the Ego is something which cannot possibly be dismissed. To argue one's self out of existence would be a mental feat reminding us of the

Kilkenny cats, or rather of the wonderful American animal which jumps down its own throat and so disappears.

But the acknowledgment of the true existence of the individual is a very different thing from the assumption of his eternal persistence. The former is a point on which I imagine we are all practically agreed, while the latter is a doctrine regarding which we shall probably be found to differ very considerably in opinion.

Stephen Fairbank.—I will only interrupt so far as to ask Dr. Stoffkraft whether he regards the desire of immortality as a grossly selfish wish. My excuse for the interruption is that if this can be proved it will greatly simplify our future discussions, if indeed it do not render them altogether superfluous.

Dr. Hermann Stoffkraft.—I do not see that the wish for a personal immortality can be regarded as something intensely selfish. I am conscious of possessing that wish myself, and yet it is not associated in my mind with any desire to promote my own happiness to the detriment of my fellows, which is the true definition of selfishness.

Stephen Fairbank.—Dr. Stoffkraft has told us that he can perceive no selfishness in the desire for immortality. I should now like to have his opinion regarding the alternative doctrine which the Comtist school would put in its place. I mean that of a posthumous unconscious life in the Cosmos—living as it were through the influence which we have exerted during our lives, and which will propagate and extend itself after we ourselves have ceased to exist and have been forgotten.

Dr. Hermann Stoffkraft.—All right-minded persons are conscious of possessing two wishes of this kind which may be separately discussed. The one is a longing for the continuation of individual existence and happiness. The other is a feeling that the truest form of happiness consists in doing good to others. Now the longing for an individual immortality may, it appears to me, be regarded as an extension of the first of these desires ; while the Comtist doctrine of a posthumous life through the Cosmos may be equally regarded as an extension of the second. But surely these two desires ought to be recognised as allies, or brethren, rather than as rivals and enemies. And, as a matter of fact, individual existence lies at the root of everything. Surely the true conception of immortality is that of a life of increased usefulness and activity indefinitely prolonged beyond the grave. And the Christian system, generously viewed, appears to lead not only to an indefinite expansion of each of these desires, but also to an increased deepening of the vital and necessary connection between the two. Surely the good man desires immortality in order that he may greatly increase his love to others, and his power of doing them good—a result which means at the same time an increased nearness to God.

No doubt we see through a glass darkly, and there have been numerous partial ways of looking at heaven. I presume that the idea of eternal praise has been borrowed very much from the apocalyptic vision, and it again from the accessories of the Jewish temple. The idea of a place of rest, on the other hand, springs naturally from the feeling of weariness which invariably accompanies a prolonged life in this world. But I particularly wish to point out the great contrast between the breadth of the Christian system, and the narrowness of the Comtist doctrine. The Christian immortality is the inheritance of the humblest individual who does his duty; of the man who has only one talent as well as of him who has ten; of the philosopher who spends his life in discovering principles, as well as of the humble village dame. On the other hand, the Comtist heaven is limited to a favoured few, including of course the great philosopher, who is pleased to think what future generations will say to his labours, but excluding the village dame, who knows perfectly well that she will have no future immortality in the Cosmos.

The Rev. Ralph Bemerton.—Dr. Stoffkraft has pointed out with much clearness that the

Comtist scheme excludes all of our race except a favoured few from the benefits of its grotesque immortality. I may be allowed to add that it gives the men of our race an undue advantage over the women. In all civilised communities there must be a very great difference between the duties performed by these two great sides of the human family.

The function of the man is rather to educate and subdue the world, while that of the woman is more directly concerned with the education of the individual. I do not, of course, mean to say that the man is not to consider the individual, or that the woman is not to regard the world, but I yet hold within certain limits to the distinction which I have drawn. And while I am quite of opinion that a freer and fuller opportunity of usefulness should be opened up to those women who can avail themselves of it, I yet clearly perceive that in any community the civilising offices of the one sex must be very different from those of the other. Therefore, any theory which cuts at the root of individual existence beyond the grave will, I feel sure, provoke a stronger resentment from the woman than from the man. In my youth I translated some German hexameters, which seem to me to illustrate this point fairly enough, though, if you will, in a rather Klopstockian vein of sentiment or sentimentality. It is strange from any point of view—strangest of all from that of Comte—that such things should haunt one for a lifetime. Here they are :—

A PHILOSOPHER'S HEXAMETERS TO HIS MISTRESS.

Mine, in clustering coils of circumstantial existence
Tracing the thread of purpose to seek for the presence of order,
Then with unfaltering hand to knit the unknitted together.
Thine a far gentler task—with imperceptible deftness
Binding invisible bonds, a hundredfold intertwining
Children and parents, and husband and wife, and household
    and country.
Whose in the social whole the nobler share and the higher
Power? the stronger effect and the fuller meed of achievement?
Dearest, the woof was spread ere yet thy assiduous fingers
Busily plied their task, nor shall it break and the worker
Sink unheeded away, with work half done in the twilight ;—
But its fulness shall come to whoso shared in the labour,
Where no labour is vain and angels are weaving with angels.

Now, one great beauty of the Christian scheme is, that while recognising and even insisting upon this essential difference, it yet puts both sides of the human family upon an equal footing before God and as regards their hopes of a future beyond the grave. On the other hand, the curse of such religions as those of Brigham Young and Comte is, that they unduly exalt and glorify those qualities which the man possesses in contradistinction to the woman. The one is an apotheosis of the physical superiority of the man over the woman, while the other is an apotheosis of his intellectual superiority, which (so far as the present argument is concerned) must be regarded as constituting nothing more than a refined and subtle form of physical predominance. Imagine for a moment what must have happened centuries ago in that ruin we have just left. Picture to yourself the life of its inmates—the mother bending over her drooping child, impressed with the mournful conviction that the earthly life of the beloved one was fast drawing to a close, but yet full of a noble and generous faith in God and of the sure and certain hope of a joyful resurrection. Think of all this, and then tell me whether this glorified maternal affection be not one of the noblest and most sacred treasures of our nature, and whether, if the hope of immortality were destroyed, it could possibly exist in the cold and withering shade of the Comtist philosophy. I utterly fail to see that it could even be imagined.

Hitherto I have been dealing with the best feelings of our nature—let me now deal with the worst, and contemplate the operation of a triumphant positivism upon the malefactor. Let us endeavour to realise the hell of the Comtists. It consists, I presume, in the dread that our evil deeds will perpetuate for us a species of degraded immortality in the Cosmos. But I need hardly tell you that the most depraved of our race are utterly indifferent to the terrors of any kind of posthumous disgrace, while many, at least, of them nevertheless stand in awe of the righteous indignation of God. Take, for instance, the successful and secret murderer. In not a few cases he has voluntarily come forward to be his own accuser—driven to confess by an inner voice which speaks to him of the judgment to come. Now, what motive would there be for such a confession under the Comtist philosophy? He has made a mistake; he is sorry for it, and will not repeat it; but why should he make a confession which must at once cut short his liberty, if not his existence? If he be a philosopher he may perhaps conclude that such a confession might ultimately tend by an indirect process somewhat to increase the happiness of the race, but being a murderer he is not likely to act upon this conviction. In fine, the Comtist system, while, on the one hand, it withdraws support from the best feelings of our nature, withdraws, on the other, all adequate and practical restraint from the indulgence of such, at least, of our vicious propensities as are not well provided against by law and police.

To conclude: I am even inclined to think that this system will act prejudicially upon its particular pet, the great philosopher, who, while babbling about a posthumous life in the Cosmos, may not unfrequently be inclined to sacrifice its empty praise for the solid pudding of a present reputation.

Sir Kenneth M'Kelpie.—There is yet another aspect of the question which must not be overlooked. No one admires more than myself the wonderful advances recently made towards exhibiting the physical unity of the Cosmos. Not only are the great masses of the universe bound together possibly by the same law of force, but they appear to be made of the same materials, and to be surrounded by the same medium. There is a strong mechanical and physical binding together of the whole by a bond whose existence we can scientifically perceive.

When, however, we leave the objective for the subjective side of the Cosmos—matter for life—we fail, unless we embrace the doctrine of immortality, to reach any adequate conception of unity. As far as mechanics and physics are concerned, the Comtist has no doubt risen to the conception of an underlying unity in the visible Cosmos, but he fails utterly to recognise any sort of intelligent intercourse between the various inhabitants; there are to him, in a sense, as many universes as there are individual existences.

I presume none of us expect science ever to realise in this world the ingenious dreams of the modern novelist, or to provide us with the means of visiting about from star to star. Thus an intelligent intercourse between the inhabitants of the various worlds depends entirely upon the possibilities of a future state. Then, again, think of those exquisite scenes of natural beauty that have all along been hidden in corners—

> . . . 'Where no one comes
> Or hath come, since the making of the world,'

and tell me if it be not more philosophical as well as pleasant to imagine that these have nevertheless been a source of joy, if not to man, yet to spiritual presences such as the angels, who may, perhaps, visit this world not entirely on errands of mercy.

Dr. Hermann Stoffkraft.—I am perfectly

willing to allow the force of all these observations.

Stephen Fairbank.—In consequence of this admission, I will now propose a question to Dr. Stoffkraft.

He has allowed that in respect of its practical working the doctrine of immortality has great advantages over any other alternative hypothesis. Now unless there be some definite proof that this doctrine is untrue, there will no doubt be always a large number of followers who will adopt it, accompanied with a religious belief which will probably be some form of Christianity. But, in virtue of the great practical excellence of this form of belief, these adherents will be placed in a position of advantage.

They will, by a species of natural selection, and on account of the suitability of their principles to the requirements of society, achieve a predominance over their opponents, and we may therefore look forward to a time when the doctrine of immortality will be universally held.

Dr. Hermann Stoffkraft.—I readily reply to

the challenge of our host. I feel sure that the doctrine is untrue, and that the clear light of science is even now penetrating into the dark corner where immortality was believed to be concealed.

It will, I feel sure, withdraw the veil from the Christian holy of holies, which will be found as great a blank as its Jewish prototype was when similarly invaded.

Stephen Fairbank.—If this be so, have we not here a very strange anomaly? By following the truth—that is to say (according to Dr. Stoffkraft), by giving up our belief in immortality—the result will be less conducive to social development than if we were to persevere in believing a lie. Nay, it is even possible that society, when sufficiently enlightened to disbelieve in a future state, will in consequence become disintegrated, and begin falling to pieces.

How does it happen that here alone misery instead of happiness, weakness instead of strength, is the result of conforming ourselves to the conditions of our environment?

Dr. Hermann Stoffkraft.—I cannot reply to this question except by saying that I must regard consciousness as a mistake, at least a consciousness sufficiently developed to feel at the same time a longing for immortality and an assurance of its impossibility. Probably the Governor of the universe has done his best; there may very possibly be an inherent contradiction in immortality; it may be as impossible to make a being immortal as to make two and three equal to six. This we do not know, but what we may easily divine, if we choose to examine for ourselves, is, that the universe around us is not so constituted as to admit of immortality. Inasmuch, however, as I ardently long for that which I feel to be impossible, I am personally put to confusion, and am reluctantly compelled to admit that the Deity has made a mistake.

Elijah Holdfast.—'Feeling sure that a doctrine is untrue' is, you will permit me to say, Doctor, what you Germans call reasoning 'nach Art der Frauen,' and, I presume, must be considered as at least virtually an acknowledgment of defeat. Had you said no more, I should not have thought it necessary to reply. But your answer to our friend Fairbank shifts the point of the discussion to a region in which I did not expect *you* to travel. I have heard such things many times, especially of late; but never till now from the lips of a true man of science. I fear I cannot answer you with the judicial calmness we ought all to display. Your last sally was so abrupt, and (again pardon me) so suggestive of the 'child crying for the moon,' that I am somewhat at a loss how to take it. What should you say if a thief, who had an intense longing for your massive gold watch, and at the same time an assurance that it was impossible to get it, should say that Providence had no doubt done its best, but had made a mistake in grafting this feeling of covetousness in him?

Or to take what many would think higher ground, what should you say to a man of pseudo-science, with an ardent desire to be distinguished as a discoverer or inventor, but who was conscious of his own incapacity to achieve for himself such a species of immortality, should he happen unguardedly to admit that Providence had no doubt done all it could for him, but had made a mistake in making him if it could not also give him genius?

Should you not punish the thief if he attempted to rob you? And as to the pseudo-scientific man, would you not say something so calm and yet so conclusive in its calmness as to wither his little soul within him?

I must really once more apologise for my frankness, but I almost fancy that your observation was a jocular attempt to find what were the limits of our endurance, and I have tried to answer you in a similar spirit.

Dr. Hermann Stoffkraft.—But, my dear sir, there is surely a great difference between the depraved appetites of certain individuals and the nearly universal craving of civilised man for a personal immortality beyond the grave. Here we have a deeply seated feeling which has conscience for its friend, while the assurance of its gratification would be attended with the most excellent results. Nevertheless it must remain ungratified if there be any truth in scientific principles.

Elijah Holdfast.—I did not quite make out from the Doctor's words that he was prepared to bring forward a scientific *proof* of the impossibility of immortality. I rather imagined that while he had on the one hand an 'unscientific feeling' of the advantage of immortality, he had on the other a 'scientific feeling' (whatever that may mean) of its impossibility. But if the Doctor has got a *proof*, that is a very different thing, and the subject is one which may be profitably discussed. Perhaps I, in my turn, may be allowed to 'feel an assurance' that when this discussion is complete, the mistake will be found to be transferred to somewhat different shoulders from those on which the Doctor supposes it now to rest.

Stephen Fairbank.—Well, well, gentlemen, we are now nearing home, and I have two remarks to make. The first is, that I am sure we shall all be delighted if Dr. Stoffkraft will give us his argument against Immortality. The second is, that in the Paradoxical Society no one is supposed to know beforehand the subject of the debate.

Dr. Hermann Stoffkraft.—Pray, my dear sir, what conclusion do you draw from these two disjointed remarks?

Stephen Fairbank.—Only this, Doctor, that we shall all look to you to open the debate in the Paradoxical.

CHAPTER III.

DOCTOR STOFFKRAFT OPENS THE DEBATE.

'GENTLEMEN,' said a conjuror, one fine starry evening, 'these heavens are a *deceptio visûs;* what you call stars are nothing but fiery motes in the air.' . . . Whereupon the artist produced a long syringe of great force; and . . . filled it with mud and dirty water, which he then squirted with might and main against the zenith. The wiser of the company unfurled their umbrellas; but most part, looking up in triumph, cried, 'Down with delusion! It is an age of science!' . . . Here the mud and dirty water fell, and bespattered and beplastered these simple persons, and even put out the eyes of several, so that they never saw the stars any more.

THOMAS CARLYLE.

AT the breakfast table next morning Sir Kenneth presented himself, punctual to the minute, and without a trace of that *négligé* which is too often tolerated even among those who have not allowed themselves to sink into effeminacy or luxury.

Holdfast and the host were already there, eagerly scanning the morning papers, so utterly absorbed in their political excitement as to pay no attention to one another, nor to Miss Fairbank, who sat watching them with some amusement. Sir Kenneth, smiling at their abstraction, engaged in a lively discussion with the young lady, and no one seemed to think of breakfast. At last Holdfast threw down the *Times*, and hastily apologising to Miss Fairbank, thus addressed Sir Kenneth :—

Elijah Holdfast.—Well, Sir Kenneth, we have carried our man after all at St. Oran. I must say I am surprised, for I could hardly conceive a worse specimen to bring forward. I told them that it was an utter mistake—that we should have to run our very best available man in order to have any chance against the Master of Glenstriven, with his many advantages of character, influence, and even clanship. They merely said, 'We know our men,' and the event has justified them. But I never could understand Scotland.

Sir Kenneth M‘Kelpie.—I am grieved, but not surprised. Were I less of a Scotsman than I am I should have given up Scotland long ago.

But painful, and even ridiculous, as I feel this last business to be, I receive it as an additional proof that things will soon mend.

Stephen Fairbank.—You were always a paradoxer, Sir Kenneth, but this is quite unintelligible to me—unless from the common point of view that when things are at the worst they begin to mend.

Sir Kenneth M'Kelpie.—Even that saying is mathematically correct. What is the definition of a minimum? But, unfortunately, it never can be applied in proper time, for things require to begin to mend before we can be sure that they have yet reached the worst. My hope is based upon better grounds, which I think I can give you in a few words.

It is all a question of education. Now there can be no doubt that the education of the average voter is in Scotland (to a small extent at least) higher than it is in England. But it is as yet far from having risen to *culture;* and, in consequence, while he has lost the semi-slavish admiration for rank, wealth, or merit which Hodge still feels, he has, in the reaction from this (and possibly by the recollection of cherished traditional wrongs) come to envy and even to *hate* his superiors in position or intellect. Remember the fate of Aristides. The average Scottish voter has just the requisite amount of education to fit him 'meanly to admire mean things.' This, if I recollect rightly, is Thackeray's definition of a snob.

Elijah Holdfast.—Thanks, Sir Kenneth. *Habemus!* We have got it this time, Fairbank, and no mistake. At any other time I could have disputed the point with you, Sir Kenneth; but this St. Oran business is really too bad. When is your national education likely to rise to culture, as you call it?

Sir Kenneth M'Kelpie.—When your 'Liberal' devices for keeping us from progressing shall have been thoroughly countermined; when every candidate for a seat on a School Board shall be required to prove that he has himself received a good education, and to show that he has not forgotten it; when our Protestant sects cease to split hairs, and once for all join cordially in those vastly more important matters in which they perfectly agree.

Elijah Holdfast.—In other words, when Scotland ceases to be Scottish.

Sir Kenneth M'Kelpie.—Remember Home's lines :—

> " Let him drink port! the English statesman cried ;—
> He drank the poison, and his spirit died."

Quaint as they are, and dealing with a trivial matter, they have an allegorical meaning which is as true as it is important.

Stephen Fairbank.—I cannot but agree with you, Sir Kenneth, though to say so is contrary to my allegiance. But here comes the Doctor! Good morning, Doctor! I hope you are in great force to-day.

Dr. Hermann Stoffkraft.—Thank you. Good morning, Miss Fairbank. I must apologise for my late appearance. But you are aware of the ordeal I have to endure to-day?

Miss Fairbank.—I was glad to hear from my brother that you are to lead the debate.

My cousin Fanny and I intend to be present; but we come to listen only, not to speak.

Dr. Hermann Stoffkraft.—It is only in churches, I think, that women are ordered to be silent; and, in our preliminary discussion yesterday, the clergyman and your father both took their stand mainly upon woman's side of the question, while Mr. Holdfast told me I was reasoning 'after the manner of women.' I think, then, that it is not improbable that you might contribute usefully to our debates.

Miss Fairbank.—Not to-day, at least, Doctor. We have yet to learn what this Paradoxical Society really is, and how its affairs are managed. Then we shall be able to judge whether we can reasonably take part in your discussions.

At this moment Frederick Fairbank and the other absentees appeared on the lawn, each with a fair basket of trout; and the company was soon seriously engaged at breakfast. The conversation, of course, became prosaic as well as discursive and fragmentary, Sir Kenneth standing up for the supreme merits of kippered salmon, while some of the others rallied him good-humouredly on the Scottish (?) partiality for sweets, particularly jam and marmalade.

After breakfast came the Doctor's turn. It was supposed to be as impossible for a German to dispense with his pipe as for a Scotsman to breakfast without marmalade, and so said the men of the party as they smoked in the garden. But he bore it all with great glee, and retorted, to the surprise of the company, by giving a singular list of non-smoking Germans, in which were to be found the names of some of the very greatest of modern scientific men.

Frederick Fairbank.—And do you consider, Doctor, that their non-smoking has anything to do with their scientific eminence?

Dr. Hermann Stoffkraft.—Nothing whatever; at least, that I have been able to trace. Smokers have indeed told me that their practice was eminently conducive to concentration of thought, inasmuch as it rendered them insensible to petty disturbances; but I have met with no facts of importance on either side of this question.

Frederick Fairbank.—Precisely my case. On every disputed question you meet with bigots and zealots without end; but their zeal is, in almost every instance, directly proportional to their ignorance.

The Rev. Ralph Bemerton (stepping up to the group).—Exactly so; it is the very opposite of the 'zeal which is according to knowledge.'

Stephen Fairbank.—Good morning, Parson. I presume we are now ready for the proper business of the day.

The Rev. Ralph Bemerton.—Which must be held in the house to-day at least: under the trees here you are in blissful ignorance of the storm which is coming up from the sea. I have been watching it as I came across the hill just now.

Punctually at 11 A.M. the whole company met in the great hall. A huge fire blazed in the grand old chimney, for already the air had become chilly.

After a few trivial remarks, each member assumed an attitude of anxious and critical attention to the Doctor.

It was a curious and interesting study to note the various modes in which men so different in character and person, though all of high and trained intellectual powers, prepared themselves for a continued mental effort.

Stephen Fairbank leant back motionless in his easy-chair, with eyes half closed, but keenly directed to the speaker. Elijah Holdfast seemed to gaze at the fretted ceiling, but in reality he was exercising his sense of hearing alone. Sir Kenneth, on the other hand, though his eyes were always wide open and directed full on the Doctor, was scarcely for a moment quiet, changing from one attitude to another with wonderful rapidity. The ladies perused the carpet, now and then only throwing a momentary glance on the speaker.

Premising that for the sake of accuracy he had committed to writing a great part of what he had to say (whether this had been done on the previous evening or not, the editors are not prepared to state with certainty), Dr. Stoffkraft opened as follows the discussion on the

'Possibility of a Future State.'

Dr. Hermann Stoffkraft.—It seems to me that, though there are at least three main points of view which may be adopted in regarding the question before us, all of them ultimately lead us to inquire into the nature of Life itself as the one chief difficulty in the discussion.

We may argue (as I propose to do) from the scientific principle of continuity, or from the moral and social point of view, or from that of religious belief in any of its thousand forms. I shall not, for the moment, give any reasons for attaching comparatively little importance to the two latter methods beyond the obvious fact of *their utter indefiniteness.* However you may regard them, I think you will at least agree with me in *this*, that that subject is not science (at least not as yet science) in which no two students can be found to exactly agree with one another even about its elementary principles.

Nothing is more painfully ludicrous to me than the way in which men, even of considerable ability, are certain to fall into what average common sense perceives to be the most palpable absurdities, as soon as they begin to lay down principles in political economy, ethics, or metaphysics. Hence probably the reason why (for nearly a century) these subjects have failed to enlist the highest class of thinkers. And, even in those religious systems whose articles, creeds, or standards are drawn up with all the minuteness and precision of which logical acumen is capable, we see by the trials for heresy (of which we have constant examples in Protestant countries) that scarcely any two followers of the same system attach exactly the same meaning to any one term of their common belief. I may have more to say on this subject, and I am quite certain, beforehand, that you will not agree with me; but I have alluded to it sufficiently to justify for the present, to my own mind at least, the course of argument which I have found it necessary to adopt. For I do not consider that any useful purpose can be served by a discussion, whatever be its subject, unless the terms which have to be employed are sufficiently definite in their generally accepted meaning to secure us against ambiguity. Many things, of which we can form only very vague conceptions, are still sufficiently indicated by a properly chosen word; while in other cases a term of excessive vagueness seems to have been introduced to help men to talk, with the appearance of knowledge, about things of which they are profoundly ignorant.

Thus the word *Infinite*, as applied to distance, duration, or measurable magnitude of any kind, suggests a perfectly definite meaning —exactly the same to all intelligent minds— though altogether beyond the grasp of any one mind, however acute.

On the other hand, the term *Cause* is one which at the first glance every one thinks he understands, and, which, therefore, he freely uses; yet where will you find two men (who think for themselves) to agree exactly in the meaning they attach to it?

Feeling so strongly as I do, upon this point, I shall endeavour to make perfectly clear the precise meaning which I attach to any somewhat doubtful word which I may be obliged to employ. And one of the most important of these presents itself at the very outset.

I attach to the term *Continuity*, when employed to denote a general scientific principle, a meaning quite distinct from those which (more or less akin to one another) it usually bears in mathematical and physical science. For in these the term simply implies the *absence of gaps or sudden changes*, which may be of many kinds. Thus, a 'continuous' line may be straight, or curved, or even zig-zag, but there must be no interruptions in it. A curve has usually 'continuous' change of direction, or, as Newton called it, continued curvature; and the want of this is the essence of zig-zag. When matter is said 'continuously' to fill any space, it is meant that there is no portion (however small) of that space which is not fully occupied by matter.

But the 'principle of continuity' implies, as I understand it, a thinkable relation, or relations, between successive or simultaneous events in the physical universe, whether in connection with what we call life or not.

In other words, it is merely a mode of stating what experience has shown to be true;—that nothing physical occurs without a physical antecedent, and that whenever all the determining circumstances are the same, the result is always the same. *Why* this happens to be the case is a point on which I have thought much, but hitherto without reaching any very definite conclusion. It, happily, however, need not occupy us just now, as all I require for the sake of my argument is the concession, which you are doubtless all ready to make, that continuity, as I have just explained it, is found by all recorded scientific experience to be a universal fact.

Elijah Holdfast.—Hold there, Doctor! I

was most unwilling to interrupt you, so I let pass several points which appeared to me to be objectionable; but I cannot allow so very grave a statement to pass except under strong protest; especially as you have assumed that we are all ready to agree to it. It seems to me that your last position explicitly denies the occurrence of any supernatural event whatever. If so, it must be considered as a begging of the whole question;—for were it granted, I cannot see the interest there would be in a future state, even if we could then allow its possibility.

Dr. Hermann Stoffkraft.—My dear sir, are you not a little hasty? I am commencing a scientific argument, and I intend to discuss it scientifically. In accordance with this purpose I can take scientific evidence alone. This I think I have closely adhered to, and therefore I once more read my statement:—' You are doubtless all ready to make the concession that continuity, as I have just explained it, is found by *all recorded scientific* experience to be a universal fact.' Is it not so?

Elijah Holdfast.—Pray go on, Doctor. I did not notice the word 'scientific,' and I shall take care not to interrupt you again.

Dr. Hermann Stoffkraft.—You are all, no doubt, well acquainted with an old, but still fairly respectable book, Paley's 'Natural Theology.' Perhaps the most hackneyed passage in it is that about the savage finding a watch. It seems to me, however, that this contains a very great deal of useful information which has not been extracted from it. So far as Paley, and I believe any of his commentators, have gone, the existence of the watch serves merely as a proof of design on the part of the (unknown) maker, or of some one under whose directions that maker wrought. And a precisely similar argument (perhaps not so convincing) is perpetually in the mouths of many who sneer at Paley and the system he was defending, when we find them tracing primæval man by chips of flint or by bones broken so as to allow extraction of the marrow. [I mention this in passing, not because it has anything to do with my argument, but because it is in itself particularly instructive as a characteristic of the pseudo-scientific man.] But extend Paley's illustration. Suppose we saw a watch suddenly start into existence. Here we should at once recognise a manifest breach of continuity. There would still remain, as complete as before, the evidence of design; but it would be design acting in a manner wholly inscrutable to human beings. It would put them to a species of intellectual confusion.

Thus we come to see that a watch or any other machine supplies us with something more than the mere argument for design. We perceive in it the evidence of design working after a thinkable method. We may perhaps understand very little about the machine or its method of working, but we know that it did not spring into existence ready made out of nothing. We know perfectly well that the materials of which it is made must have existed in the universe before they were brought together by the maker. Think of the spring alone. We can trace the steel back in thought to the time when it was extracted as ore of iron from the mine, or possibly when it was cut from a lump of meteoric iron, and by a number of artificial processes reduced to its present form and properties. We go still farther back and picture to ourselves the materials of which the earth is composed, gradually condensing together from what it is common to call a 'nebulous' state, cooling through long ages, and finally arriving at the disposition in which we find them now; and we can see in thought an outlying straggler of the same or of another nebulous mass, under the action of ordinary gravitation, assuming an orbit which, after millions of years, leads to its encountering the earth and forming a comparatively recent addition to its mass. All this, however, is familiar to every one of us from quite recent discussions, so that I need not enlarge on it. This is, in fact, the origin and growth of worlds, with their satellites and their primary, so far as we yet know them. But what I desire to consider specially, for its bearing on my argument, is their decay and end. I fully agree with the modern theory of the dissipation of energy, so far at least as it is predicated of any finite portion of the material universe. It follows that a time must come when life, under any conditions conceivable to us, will be physically impossible. What then? I leave this question for the present with the brief remark that, somehow or other, it would appear to suggest that such life as we are acquainted with is limited in duration, not only as regards the individual but as regards the race—and this whether we consider the vegetable or the animal creation. And with the human race must perish, of course, all that has most proudly distinguished them from the lower animals. It is not merely 'the dust of Alexander stopping a bunghole;' all the conceits of Shakspere and the stupendous discoveries of Newton must alike perish, along with the subject-matter of both. Said I not rightly but yesterday, that consciousness is a mistake?

But then it is argued that two effete suns, after practically endless ages, may impinge on one another with a terrific crash, reproducing (on a larger scale than before) the nebulous state from which worlds originally condensed, and that, as there is an infinite amount of matter in the universe, this reformation of worlds may go on without end, always on a grander scale than before. Be it so: what then? A mere repetition of the same brief and melancholy history of a world of petty inhabitants, with occasional outbursts of vast intellect, whose productions are soon to be as if they had never been, and high aspirations checked and quenched almost as soon as formed. Will you *now* tell me that consciousness is not a mistake?

But it has been said that, in all this alternate decay and rejuvenescence of habitable worlds, there is one kind of matter at least which is for ever unchangeable in its associations—which is not sporadically distributed in infinite space, but fills it throughout to the *flammantia mœnia mundi.* That life, when it seems to us to leave our material bodies, remains as truly as ever associated with the ether which everywhere freely pervades them, is a doctrine which I have often heard advanced. It is obvious that, were this doctrine capable of justification, a species of future existence would be possible. To this speculation I have given my best attention; and I think with the result of satisfactorily refuting it. It would, I fancy, lead me into too many purely scientific considerations were I now to give you my argument on this head, but it is ready at any time for such of you as care to hear it. I pass this speculation, therefore, with the one remark, that it cuts both ways, and gives quite as strong an argument for a *previous* as for a *future* disembodied existence. And this, I think, will of itself, to most men, form an insuperable objection. For it is obvious to the majority of us that we have no consciousness of a previous state of existence; and therefore the being, who might be supposed to be formed by my life associated with the ether, would have no consciousness of me—could not therefore be myself.

Having thus cleared the way, I proceed to show briefly the conclusions to which I have been led in studying the nature of consciousness.

The first step to a clear understanding of this phenomenon is furnished by the effects of so-called *Anæsthetics*. These in all cases temporarily modify, sometimes wholly destroy for a time, what we call consciousness. Now I think this one fact, which seems to be strangely overlooked by most reasoners on the subject, is of immense importance. No one in his senses can assert that an anæsthetic is anything more than ordinary matter—at least I am not aware of any which are applied in association with what we ordinarily call life. Can consciousness then be conceived to be anything but a result of some collocation or association of matter, when it is known to be modified, and in many cases wholly suspended, by the mere introduction of other matter?

This leads us to the temporary, entire or partial, loss of consciousness which we experience in *Sleep*. The normal cause of sleep is simply fatigue, the exhaustion of muscular and nervous energy in the body, again due to a mere change of collocation or association of matter. When the energy supplied by the food has had time to make good the waste, the brain matter has recovered its normal grouping, and consciousness reappears.

Now the extraordinary connection which is shown by various physiological experiments to exist between thought and brain-changes, and which is still more forcibly impressed on us by almost all the physical phenomena accompanying *Mental disease*, seems to me to prove, beyond reasonable doubt, that consciousness, and *à fortiori* life, depend upon the grouping of matter in the brain and nerve. It is commonly said that certain kinds of matter, such as phosphorus, are exclusively so associated. This I cannot help regarding as a breach of continuity. Hence, consistently with that great principle, I feel myself compelled to believe that *all kinds of matter have their motions associated with certain simple sensations:* in other words, all matter is, in some occult sense, *alive.* And just as the simpler physical properties of the atom, which we cannot even see, are lost in the complex physical properties of an aggregate such as a crystal, which we can handle and submit to experiment, so the simple life of the individual atom escapes our observation, while in the aggregate of brain atoms we recognise it as conscious existence.

I pass briefly to the remaining part of my reasoning. When this world condensed from its nebulous state the chance of the occurrence of any one special grouping of atoms must have been large, unless it was a particularly complex one. Hence we may easily see the great probability that many groups would be formed in such a way as to develop in a high degree life and consciousness such as we recognise. And just as we know that the tiniest crystal, introduced into a supersaturated solution of the same salt, suffices to multiply copies of itself without number—so we may imagine these conscious groups to be in certain circumstances capable of inducing the requisite condition for the aggregation of others similar to themselves. Such arrangements would thus have an advantage over others in the struggle for existence, and would grow not merely in numbers but in individual complexity. We have thus the first beginnings of the struggle for life. The rest you know from Wallace and Darwin.

To conclude: It is allowed on all hands that life is always found associated with energy. In fact even the most tranquil consciousness is dependent for its maintenance upon perpetual transformations of energy. Now the first law of energy tells us that none of it can either come into or leave the universe. It may pass, no doubt, from ordinary matter to ether, or from ether to ordinary matter, these two being the constituents of the universe—the bricks and mortar by the union of which the vast pile is built together. But there is nothing else to which it can go, if the theory of energy be true.

But if life *must* always be associated with energy, and is inconceivable in the ether, the only possible conclusion is that there can be no forms of living creature existence except those with which we are acquainted, and others essentially similar to them. I feel therefore bound by the principle of continuity to regard the universe before me as eternal, both as to its past and its future duration, and, believing it to be eternal, I must also regard it as infinite, if the dissipation of energy is allowed to be true. What we are thus presented with is an endless recurring series of the formation, the destruction, and the reconstitution of worlds, each world during its short history developing a race of conscious beings like ourselves, who, far from being immortal as individuals, are even more perishable than the system of which they form an exceedingly small part.

My statement is confessedly incomplete. In the rapid treatment of so vast a subject it is not possible to do more than mention the various branches of the argument. Which of them you may be inclined to agree with, which dispute, I am by no means certain. I have therefore contented myself with little beyond a bare enumeration, reserving more detailed explanation for those points only on which we may not be found in accord.

During the latter part of the Doctor's address the noise of the approaching storm had made it necessary for him to raise his voice, and the darkness had become so great that he could scarcely see his manuscript. These circumstances at last excited the Doctor and induced him to 'improve the occasion,' a method of procedure which, in the opinion of all sensible people, should be confined to parsons and lawyers, and even by them employed with the greatest caution. When he had finished the reading of his manuscript he remarked that had he lived in a rude age or amongst uninformed people the thunderstorm might have been regarded as an intimation that the powers of Nature were displeased with his doctrine. This of course would be rank Fetishism; and he would not now argue the point whether or not some such feeling lay at the root of all religions. He would rather take it for granted that none of his present audience could for a moment imagine that the connection between his speech and the thunderstorm was one of cause and effect, or that the coincidence in point of time could be anything else than accidental. Not yet thoroughly understood, the storm was merely one of the most striking of the many peculiar freaks played by water-substance in passing from one to another of its Protean forms. 'I fail altogether,' he said, 'to see in what respect lightning is more remarkable than cloud, or rain, or hail, all being mere direct physical results of evaporation and condensation of that very prosaic stuff—water. Dangerous it is, no doubt, but not more so than such vile matter as a chimney-can or a flower-pot which have a few yards to fall on your head. And if one wishes to be altogether free from danger in a thunderstorm, he has only to dress himself in an old suit of armour, discarded long ago as useless against that villainous gunpowder, but a perfect protection from the bolts of Diespiter. The one, perhaps you may say, was the invention of a monk, the other of a pagan. But this would be the very climax of unfair argument.'

A dazzling blaze of lightning seemed to linger for a moment in the hall, followed immediately by a sharp crack of thunder, apparently close overhead, and then silence. Some of the company felt almost stunned, and all agreed that they had had an exceedingly narrow escape. Fairbank and his son at once ran out to inspect the premises, and to provide promptly against any possible danger from fire. But nothing seemed to be injured, at least so much as to require immediate attention, so they returned to the hall. It had been the last effort of the storm. In a very few minutes the summer sun was shining brightly overhead, and the birds were singing merrily on the dripping branches.

The Doctor, in congratulating the party on their lucky escape, took occasion to ask the host whether he imagined that he (the Doctor) had already been answered. The smiling host informed the good-natured Doctor that on the contrary he had given them some very hard nuts to crack, which however they must try to attack after lunch.

Here Sir Kenneth could not resist whispering audibly to the Doctor, 'I was never so convinced of the existence of elemental spirits as I have been to-day. But they did not treat you well, Doctor. Now don't tell me that it was not done on purpose—don't pretend that it was only a coincidence.'

The Doctor had no time to reply, for at this very moment he was requested to lead Miss Fairbank in to lunch.

CHAPTER IV.

THE REPLY.

'So they had them to the top of a high hill called Clear, and gave them the glass to look.' *The Pilgrim's Progress.*

AFTER lunch the ladies informed the company that owing to their home engagements they could not attend the Paradoxical any more that day, whereupon the host suggested a walk, as the afternoon was likely to prove fine.

If they were not afraid of eight miles he would show them something very curious, and they might continue their discussion by the way. (*Agreed to.*) He would begin by thanking the Doctor for his discourse, and more especially for Paley's watch, and the mode in which he had introduced it.

Dr. Hermann Stoffkraft.—I am glad you agree with me that the hypothesis of the sudden coming into being of a watch would put all finite intellects to permanent confusion.

Stephen Fairbank.—I quite agree with you, Doctor, and feel disposed to push the argument even further. Suppose, for instance, some one were to suggest as an alternative hypothesis the infinite past duration of the watch, what now should *you* say to such a view?

Dr. Hermann Stoffkraft.—It would be no improvement. You would not by this means get rid of intellectual confusion. In the case before us you are compelled by your intellect to try to imagine how the parts of the watch were brought together; but the hypothesis of eternity pulls you up with a vengeance. I must have a previous state, and this must be a conceivable one—somehow or other in the universe, and not out of it.

Stephen Fairbank.—Well, Doctor, you have completely disposed of the eternity hypothesis. But imagine that some very pertinacious objector (like Frederick there) were next to suggest that the watch might have been formed by the operation of blind natural forces, such as those which round the pebbles on a beach, what should you say in reply to this?

Dr. Hermann Stoffkraft.—I should say, 'How absurd!' Blind natural forces do not act in this uniform manner; they can turn out rounded stones no doubt, but these are irregular and of different sizes. They don't turn out watches, or engravings, or complex products accurately moulded. These are only produced by intelligent agents operating in the universe and designing uniformity.

Stephen Fairbank.—Many thanks, my dear Doctor, I see we are all perfectly agreed about the watch. Now, let me take another instance, and ask if you would object to regard the Sun as eternal?

Dr. Hermann Stoffkraft.—Undoubtedly I should. My objection to the sun's eternity is twofold, one derived from scientific principle and one from the scientific facts called the laws of energy. Let us take the last first. I can no more imagine a finite body like the sun to have been giving out light and heat at a finite rate from all eternity than I can imagine a candle to have been burning from all eternity. Again, my objection from scientific principle is that the sun, equally with the watch, is a collocation of matter in space, and I am therefore bound to imagine an antecedent state out of which it was educed.

Stephen Fairbank.—I suppose, however, you will allow that the sun has been brought into its present state through the operation of natural forces, while the watch is produced by an intelligent agent designing uniformity.

Dr. Hermann Stoffkraft.—Precisely so. But of course, I do not mean to say that the moulding of the sun does not imply design. I only assert that it has been brought about by that which we call 'Nature,' while the watch has been brought about by that which we call 'Art.'

The Rev. Ralph Bemerton.—In the language

of Sir Kenneth's compatriots, I 'take instruments and crave extracts.' But for use at a future stage only, as I do not wish to interrupt the present run of the discussion.

Stephen Fairbank.—Just one word more, then, on this branch of our subject. Suppose the savage of Paley had found a hundred or a thousand watches, or even many thousands, all of the same pattern, would this weaken your argument?

Dr. Hermann Stoffkraft.—On the contrary, it would strengthen it. For, to take a simpler case, when I see a schoolboy's marble, for instance, I cannot tell whether this may not have been formed by Nature, but when I see a thousand all of nearly the same pattern, I am quite sure that they have been made by man.

Stephen Fairbank.—Now, a few questions on another point :—I suppose we are all agreed that molecules and atoms form the material basis of the present universe, or, to adopt a well-known analogy, they are the bricks out of which the structure is built, while the ether may be compared to the cement by means of which these various bricks are built together. Do you imagine, Doctor, that these bricks were originally of different sizes and shapes?

Dr. Hermann Stoffkraft.—Without pretending to dogmatise, I am rather inclined to adopt the hypothesis of Prout and Lockyer, and to imagine that the primordial atoms were all of the same pattern, in which case the great variety of chemical substances we possess would be due to varied groupings of these atoms more or less intimate, the strongest or most self-contained groupings forming what we now call elements, simply because we are unable to tear their components asunder. I look upon these primordial atoms as very small bodies capable of intensely rapid vibrations, and always in motion.

Stephen Fairbank.—I suppose you would object to the hypothesis which regards them as having been created in time out of nothing?

Dr. Hermann Stoffkraft.—Most decidedly,

for would not this (even without the supposition that they were created from nothing) put the intellect to permanent confusion?

Stephen Fairbank.—I quite agree with you. Now, what do you say to their eternity? For my own part I cannot regard them as eternal, my objections being twofold, and very similar to those you have advanced against the eternity of the sun. One is from the theory of energy, for since the dissipation of cosmical energy is accompanied *pari passu* with the aggregation of mass, I should expect to meet with very large if not infinite masses in a physical universe that was at once eternal and infinite. The other is derived from scientific principle, for I must conceive the atom as truly as the sun to represent a collocation of something in space. Indeed it is certain that the structure of the atom, not to speak of that of the molecule, is vastly more complex than that of any watch—*quâ* watch. The same reasoning should therefore apply to both, and I am thus led to some anterior conceivable state in virtue of which the existence of the atom was brought about.

Dr. Hermann Stoffkraft.—My dear sir, what can I do? It is a choice between two evils (forced upon me by that lamentable mistake, Consciousness), and of the two I would rather regard the atom as eternal than as created in time. No, no, development is a good horse—a very good horse—but it must not be ridden too hard.

During this utterance, which seemed to be *extracted* from him rather than spontaneously spoken, the Doctor was visibly excited, and relieved himself by whirling his umbrella rapidly round and round his head.

In the midst of one of these revolutions a sudden thought struck the worthy Doctor, and that particular gyration was not properly completed.

The result was serious, for the umbrella, narrowly missing the head of Sir Kenneth, came sharply in contact with the rim of his hat. This unexpected assault sent the knight's headpiece high in air, and might have given rise to a chase more than usually long and laborious, inasmuch as the party were ascending a rather steep slope. But Frederick Fairbank was a cricketer, and 'fielded' it with singular promptitude, restoring the hat to its owner almost as soon as he became aware of his loss.

Meanwhile the worthy Doctor, utterly unconscious of the mischance, was seen eagerly working up and down one of those india-rubber rings which formed, two years since, an invariable appendage to all umbrellas.

As the knight was about to ask the meaning of this strange performance, the host, by way of diversion, thought it absolutely necessary to say something.

Stephen Fairbank.—What is it all about, Doctor? What is the matter with your umbrella?

Sir Kenneth M'Kelpie.—There is a great deal the matter. It has demolished my hat, narrowly missing my head, and now, if I mistake not, it is just about to demolish the doctrine of the soul's immortality!

Dr. Hermann Stoffkraft.—I most particularly beg your pardon, Sir Kenneth. Gentlemen all, pray receive my apology—I was indeed carried away for the moment, but I think I have made a hit.

Frederick Fairbank (aside).—So you did, but you were had at slip!

Dr. Hermann Stoffkraft.—Now (*turning to Stephen Fairbank*), what do you think of the notion, due to one of your own physicists, that the material universe has been developed by vortex motion out of the ether, or of some other fluid filling the whole of space? I confess I was reminded of this by noticing the india-rubber ring of my umbrella, which you all know represents a vortex ring very well.

Stephen Fairbank.—Developed out of the ether or some other fluid! How or by whom? Surely not by intelligent beings residing in the ether or other fluid, for you told us in your discourse there could be no life there.

Dr. Hermann Stoffkraft.—I meant, rather, developed by the Deity.

Stephen Fairbank.—But would not this be an action in time from without the universe, thus putting the intellect to confusion? It would imply an abrupt and inexplicable starting up in the Universe, not exactly of matter, but of energy; for I presume one can hardly imagine the ether or other fluid having a natural propensity suddenly to develop vortex rings of its own accord.

Dr. Hermann Stoffkraft (reflecting).—You are right—it would. So there must have been a prior universe different from the ether, out of which the present system has been evolved—(*after a pause*)—suppose we call it the Unseen Universe.

Stephen Fairbank (smiling).—The name will do very well. Now as we are agreed that the visible universe must have been developed from the Unseen, I will ask you to go a step further. For the Unseen universe, no less than the seen, is an object of intellectual vision—represents in fact a collocation of some sort, and hence it too must have been developed out of a previous state.

Dr. Hermann Stoffkraft.—I see now what you are aiming at. You are driving me back to Universe after Universe, to process after process, forming together an illimitable avenue, and you are quite determined we shall never get to the end.

Stephen Fairbank.—You could not have expressed my meaning more clearly. What have you or I, my dear Doctor, to do with the end or the bottom of things?

If the principle of continuity demands that no limits shall be set to time and space, does it not equally demand that there shall be no bounds to structural complexity? Whenever you become intellectually aware of anything existing in the Universe, you at once ask yourself three questions: When did it arise? where did it arise? and out of what did it arise? And an anonymous modern writer compares time, space, and structural complexity to three independent co-ordinates, in terms of which the process of development goes on simultaneously as our sphere of knowledge is enlarged.[1]

Dr. Hermann Stoffkraft.—Good! I like the idea, but of course we cannot now regard the atom as an extremely simple thing.

Stephen Fairbank.—Certainly not; on the contrary, we must regard it as only less complex than the whole universe.

The party were now almost scrambling upwards, and it was at length evident whither their host was leading them. Elmsly House was seen far below on the slope of the valley, shut in by a range of somewhat lofty hills. These were very even in elevation and outline, with the exception of a little gap towards which they were rapidly approaching. In a short time they had almost reached the entrance of the gap, and here the host asked them to rest for a moment, to look back upon the valley from which they had ascended.

---

[1] *Unseen Universe*, p. 237.

The view was of a somewhat mixed and sombre character; palpable traces of the morning's storm still lingered about it, and the sky, though not altogether obscured, was yet heavily veiled by ill-defined clouds.

When he thought they had sufficiently studied the scene, Stephen Fairbank took the Doctor's arm and said, 'Now for the other side of the shield!'

In a few moments the Doctor suddenly stopped and uttered an exclamation of the most joyful surprise. No wonder he was delighted with the view which had in a moment burst upon him! There can be few sights equalling, or even rivalling it, either in this country or anywhere else.

Suddenly, at a turning-point, the party saw before them a new and glorious valley beyond the gap, with a cloudless sky above, and bathed in all the brightness and freshness of a summer afternoon, when there is 'clear shining after rain.' The Doctor had to look back repeatedly before he could assure himself that the valley he had just left was not a dream, and then again he would look forward as if afraid this new and glorious valley should after all prove to be a delusion.

When the party had sufficiently regaled themselves with the enjoyment of this delightful spectacle, the host led the way homewards, and lost no time in resuming the discussion.

Stephen Fairbank.—I would next ask you, Doctor, whether we are not carried back to an Unseen Universe by the study of the forces of the present system just as truly as when we study its origin. Let us take, for instance, the force of gravity, and try to imagine from what source it springs. That it acts at a distance without the intervention of something between the attracting masses was inconceivable to Newton, and I am sure we shall not be inclined to dispute his verdict. To regard this force as the immediate operation of the Great First Cause would surely break the principle of continuity. But if gravity acts through some sort of machinery, this must certainly be sought for in the Unseen World.

We need not now discuss the hypothesis of Le Sage and Thomson:—sufficient for our purpose that this or any other hypothesis must drive us at once to the Unseen, which must therefore be looked upon as the antecedent not only of the materials of the present system, but also of the various transmutations of energy which are continually taking place around us. And to complete our hypothesis, we must imagine the vital phenomena of the present universe to be derived from the Unseen just as truly as its objective realities. Swedenborg held, it is well known, views of this nature, and it now appears that such views are fully borne out by those scientific principles which lead us to regard the whole visible system of things (including its life phenomena) as only a fringe, and but a small fringe of that great garment of God which we may call THE UNIVERSE.

Dr. Hermann Stoffkraft.—All this may be very true, but I fail to see what proof it gives us of the soul's immortality.

Stephen Fairbank.—We will come to that presently; but I think you must own, Doctor, that your proof of the impossibility of this doctrine no longer holds good. For this was founded on the belief that there is nothing but matter and ether, and that life is impossible in ether. Now, you have already acknowledged that the Unseen is very different from the ether as we know it.

Dr. Hermann Stoffkraft.—Until you have proved to me, or at least given me good grounds for believing, that intelligence is capable of residing in the Unseen, I am surely entitled to imagine that it does not there exist.

Stephen Fairbank.—I presume we are all driven by the principle of continuity to conclude that life of some sort resides in the Unseen. And at the present stage of our argument it is at least as much an assumption to assert that such life must be very much lower than ours as it would be to assert that it must be very much higher. At present we must imagine ourselves to be in complete ignorance of the rank of this life.

Dr. Hermann Stoffkraft.—Well, we are agreed there must be life in the Unseen, of the nature of which, let us say, we are ignorant. Let us therefore confine ourselves to those points where possibly the Unseen has come in contact with ourselves, and try to discover whether they afford us any means of judging of the nature of that life which resides in the Unseen.

Stephen Fairbank.—By all means—let us do so.

Dr. Hermann Stoffkraft.—Now, as the visible universe was developed from the Unseen, and as development implies a progress from less to more complex, I conclude that life exists in the Unseen in an extremely simple state, even simpler than that which continuity leads me to associate with the atom and *a fortiori* much simpler than life as we recognise it in the human being.

Stephen Fairbank.—Your statement, Doctor,

is somewhat obscure. To make things clear let us separate between the objective or material and the subjective or life side of the visible universe.

Now, have you tried to realise how the matter of the visible universe was developed from the Unseen?

Dr. Hermann Stoffkraft.—Well, there was something or other which by virtue of the forces with which it was endowed suddenly developed into the visible universe, and this something had I suppose in like manner been previously developed out of something else, and —— so on.

Stephen Fairbank.—A very satisfactory series of processes, and very much like what matter is in the habit of doing!

Dr. Hermann Stoffkraft.—You are laughing at me I know, but is it possible to conceive of any other development?

Stephen Fairbank.—You have told us of a dead development, but is it not possible to conceive of a living one? May we not imagine that the visible universe was formed by an Intelligence residing in the Unseen, and acting through conceivable processes while developing that which we see around us?

Dr. Hermann Stoffkraft.—What a singular Being—what an unlikely existence! I entertain an invincible repugnance to believe in such a development, and should very much prefer what you are pleased to call a dead development.

Elijah Holdfast.—This won't do, Doctor. An 'invincible repugnance' to a doctrine is very closely allied to an 'assurance that it is untrue.' Both are, to my mind at least, essentially unscientific. For a man of science ought, I think, to be perfectly willing and ready to receive whatever is sufficiently demonstrated, and to take to *avizandum* all that is plausible:— his own feelings and prepossessions notwithstanding. How is knowledge to advance if your school have an invincible repugnance to a living development, while our host and the parson and their school have an equally unconquerable repugnance to a dead one? But I wrong them, for though they may feel it they will not express it, still less will they permit it to influence their judgment. But I need lay no stress on this just now:—you have already accepted the argument from analogy, and it is too late to retreat upon repugnances. The question, as it seems to me, is now simply this:—Do atoms, so far as we know their properties, suggest a dead or a living development?

The Rev. Ralph Bemerton.—Yes; I think that, for the moment, we are confronted with this question; and I should be glad to hear it discussed.

Dr. Hermann Stoffkraft.—By all means: but let my antagonist lead off.

Stephen Fairbank.—If this question be referred to scientific analogy, it is soon settled. The atom is unquestionably a compound structure, as far as the human intellect can grasp it; the primordial atoms were probably all of the same type (at least the Doctor is rather inclined to imagine they were), and they were certainly produced in enormously great numbers.

The case is precisely that of the savage who finds many thousand watches, and the Doctor has justly told us how very absurd it would be to suppose these to have arisen through mere natural operations without the aid of an intelligent being designing uniformity.

I should now like to ask the Doctor if he has at all conceived of the way in which the life of the universe was developed from the Unseen. For it appears to me that here especially we come very near to the question upon which our discussion has been founded: and that, in fact, the possibility of a future life will impress itself upon different minds in a manner, and to an extent of conviction, closely corresponding to the view taken of the origin of life itself.

Dr. Hermann Stoffkraft.—The Unseen must have possessed life—in some primitive and simple form no doubt: continuity requires so much; but the form of its life must have been even more simple than that of the atom which is a development from the Unseen. I have already, in my opening remarks, stated my belief that when the universe of atoms had sufficiently condensed together from its nebulous state, there would be a great probability that many groups would be formed in such a way as to develop in a high degree that life and consciousness which we recognise, and that such arrangements would thus have an advantage over others in the struggle for existence, and would grow not merely in numbers, but in individual complexity. The rest you know from Wallace and Darwin.

Stephen Fairbank.—But we know also from these authorities and from the universal consensus of all biologists, that no organised being which we can recognise can be produced except from an organised antecedent. Now any theory of the origin of recognised life from within this universe must take account of this law. For just as there are strong scientific grounds for believing in the existence of the atom, and in the law of the conservation of energy, so there are grounds almost equally strong for believing in the law that life, as we perceive it, can only be produced from a living antecedent. But your school, Doctor, while they hold rigidly to the atom and to energy, break the law of Biogenesis without the smallest scruple.

Dr. Hermann Stoffkraft.—In this case there can be no hypothesis at all as to the origin of recognised life from within our universe, if we assume that what we may call its natural operations do not produce life except out of a living antecedent.

Stephen Fairbank.—*Ne sutor ultra crepidam* must be our motto here, as elsewhere, and if we are to agree at all, we must take the universe *as we know it.* We will only own our missing Princess by her ability to put on the glass slipper she has left behind. You have brought us her step-sister, Doctor, and as you cannot enlarge the slipper, you are trying to break it in order to give a chance to your goddess with the splay feet.

Dr. Hermann Stoffkraft.—But, my dear Sir,

you will surely allow that the sudden production of a peculiar kind of life in the universe would break the principle of continuity.

Stephen Fairbank.—Not if it were an introduction from an Unseen of whose existence and power we were previously aware.

I feel myself compelled to look to this Unseen for the origin not only of the matter of the Visible Universe, but also of its life, for there is no other hypothesis that does not break some intellectual principle or some scientific law. Indeed, we appear to have two developments from the Unseen, the one taking place after the other, and the latter or life development, even more than the former or matter development, leading us to recognise an intelligent and spiritual Unseen.[1] And not only does your hypothesis break the law of Biogenesis, but it

---

[1] This appears to have been suggested by Jean Paul Richter, who says (*Levana*), 'At least two miracles or revelations remain for you uncontested in this age, which deadens sound with unreverberating material. They resemble an Old and a New Testament, and are these: the birth of Finite Being and the birth of Life within the hard wood of matter.'

leads you to recognise in the various orders of the eternal Unseen Universe nothing but a rudimentary form of life which we can never grasp, except in a dim intellectual way, with our present powers, and which, therefore, according to your theory, we shall never be fit to grasp at all. You thus present us with two universes, a visible one, in which we may verify phenomena, and a tremendous Unseen, which our intellect drives us to acknowledge, but with the substance or life of which we shall never be brought into more intimate contact.

The Rev. Ralph Bemerton.—If I mistake not, the Doctor in our first discussion made what I thought a very apt comparison between the life progress of the individual and that of the world, and biologists, we know, insist strongly on the very intimate likeness between the two.

Now it appears to me that this comparison has taken into account one side only of the life development. In all living things, whether animal or vegetable, we have two sides; there is first the descent from a parent or parents, and there is secondly and subsequently the ascent of the individual. To complete the analogy, we must therefore imagine that the life of our globe has somehow descended to it just as the life of the individual has in some way descended to him. A continuous life ascent from all eternity taken alone, as the Doctor will have it, is, I maintain, a fatally one-sided and incomplete hypothesis.[1]

---

[1] A writer on Evolution in the *Church Quarterly Review* (July 1878) has made an exceedingly valuable suggestion in comparing together the life history of the individual and that of the Earth. He conceives that just as in the generation of the higher organisms we have two distinct stages, one from the germ to the birth, the other from the birth to the maturity of the animal, so likewise may there be two corresponding stages in the Evolution of the life of the Earth. Again, he observes that after birth the animal develops according to quite a different set of influences from those which surround it before birth, and that a study of the one of these two developments would throw little light upon the other. So it may be, he goes on to say, that a study of the laws which now regulate the development of the life of the Earth may throw little light upon the nature of its earlier life history. It will be seen that this suggestion, taken in connection with that of Mr. Bemerton, completes the analogy between embryology and life Evolution.—(ED.)

Sir Kenneth M'Kelpie.—I see you are drawing very rapidly towards my view, that we must have always two ways of regarding an eternal development.

Now if the visible universe has emerged from a spiritual Unseen extending throughout a past eternity, is it not more natural to couple this with the development of the individual extending onwards and upwards throughout the future?

A similar thought seems to have occurred to Renan, who thus expresses himself in his dialogues and philosophical fragments:—

'It is not impossible,' he tells us, 'that in the infinitude of time the universe may minister to the perceptions and enjoyments of one single being: thus personal monotheism would be a truth. On this condition it is even possible to conceive the resurrection of individuals. The universe, reduced to one single absolute being, will be the complete life of all—the renewal of beings who have disappeared.'

He has thus, I think, brought before us,

albeit in a somewhat obscure and mystical way, the future half of the great problem, and in doing so he has, without doubt, borrowed largely from St. John.

The Rev. Ralph Bemerton.—Without pretending to discuss the merits of this somewhat obscure statement, let me briefly express my opinion upon the drift of our present argument. Whether we take the material or the life of the visible universe, I do think we are led by strong analogies to regard the Unseen as replete with spiritual power, inasmuch as it has developed and now sustains the present order. We cannot tell from the results of science whether a future has been prepared for man, but we are surely led to ask if the Unseen has given us any information on a point so important to our well-being, while we should hold ourselves prepared, at the same time, to receive proofs of this with all humility.

Dr. Hermann Stoffkraft.—I am willing to acknowledge the possibility of a Spiritual Unseen, but I strongly object to the generally received proofs of such a communication, and I do so not on one only but on many grounds. One of these alone need be mentioned now; but it is very appropriate in the present connection. In the supposed revelation to which you allude, man is treated like a child, not like an intellectual being, and the so-called proofs are asserted occurrences which, if they do not put the intellect to permanent confusion, are yet totally opposed to the mode in which Nature is known habitually to work.

Elijah Holdfast.—You will allow me to say, Doctor, that though from your point of view you speak, as you always do, with courtesy— yet from the point of view of the rest of this company, it appears altogether outrageous to speak of the Christian revelation as if it were of the same class as the mere human dogmas of various schools of philosophy. I hope the time will never come when, at least in any British company, such a classification will be tolerated. I repeat that from your point of view no exception can be taken to your mode of putting matters; but Britons, at least, are not accustomed to hear their religion calmly discussed as something on a par with Aristotle, or even with Plato.

But, to pass from this, I would ask you whether the acquisition of mere human knowledge does not depend very much upon the exercise of qualities closely approximating to the humility and receptiveness of a child.

For long ages the schoolmen tried to imagine what Nature ought to be, and science has only developed since men have been content to take things as they are. Why have you, yourself, Doctor, succeeded so greatly as a man of science? Is it not because you have taken up the study of the Universe as a little child?

Imagine a little man saying to his father :—Father, I have a profound conviction that you mean well, and I hear that you have provided a ship that is to carry me to an unknown land. I much desire, however, that you would give me a proof of the sterling qualities of this ship such as I and men of my standing (here the little atom tries to look big) may intellectually comprehend. Are the timbers thick enough, the bolts well riveted, and are there no sunken rocks in the way? Have you a sufficient supply of coals, and, above all, is the engine well greased and free from priming? Now what should you say to all this, Doctor? I know what I should do—I should promptly pull the ears of the wretched little prig. You may perhaps think me irreverent, but I cannot refrain. The matter is one on which I feel very strongly.

The Rev. Ralph Bemerton.—I quite agree with the views expressed so forcibly by my friend Mr. Holdfast, because, as you all know, I deprecate the artificial separation between the Natural and the Revealed. All is nature and all is revelation. For convenience' sake, no doubt, we set apart a particular body of knowledge which refers to the ordinary processes going on around us, whether of matter or life, and call it science, so that the laws of science are, by definition, those laws which regulate ordinary phenomena. It is thus abundantly evident that the laws of science will give us nothing more than a knowledge of the ordinary working of the Universe around us, and that if there have been communications from an intelligent Unseen giving us information which it is desirable we should possess, these will not be proved by scientific laws, inasmuch as these latter mean an artificially selected body of knowledge having exclusive reference to the ordinary working of the visible universe. We must in fact take care that we do not treat revelation like the prophet's book :—' And the vision of all is become unto you as the words of a book that is sealed, which men deliver to one that is learned, saying, Read this, I pray thee : and he saith, I cannot; for it is sealed : and the book is delivered to him that is not learned, saying, Read this, I pray thee : and he saith, I am not learned.'[1]

Stephen Fairbank.—We are now nearing

---

[1] Isaiah xxix. 11-12.

home, and I think I hear the dinner-bell, so, as chairman, I will give you leave to get ready to join the ladies within half-an-hour.

At dinner the Doctor was observed to be very absent. His usual ceremonious courtesy was scarcely able to carry him through it with decency. 'Hard hit, poor beggar,' said Frederick Fairbank to himself, 'I must back him up a little.' As he thought this the Doctor's eye met his, and read there the sympathy for which he longed. Further discussion was out of the question for that evening—indeed it was forbidden. Stephen Fairbank had said the day was sufficient for the work of men's intellects, the evening barely so for the higher duties of their hearts. But Frederick took the first opportunity of asking the Doctor to meet him early next morning for a little private talk. 'I was not quite satisfied,' he said, 'that to-day's discussion was altogether fair, and I have somewhat to tell you about it.' Dr. Stoffkraft eagerly grasped his hand, and retired on the plea of slight fatigue.

Miss Fairbank.—Now for the mystery; I wish no arguments or discussions, but it is plain to me that Dr. Stoffkraft does not think he has been quite fairly used to-day. What have you been saying or doing to him?

Stephen Fairbank.—We took no unfair advantage—though with a man of Stoffkraft's erudition one is tempted to use every means in his power. The Doctor has not yet heard of the *Unseen Universe*, and we plied him with a few arguments drawn from it.

The Rev. Ralph Bemerton.—And with equal effect and justice. He was evidently quite unprepared for an attack from the purely scientific side.

Miss Fairbank.—Of course, you let him fancy that these were your own arguments? I call that scarcely fair.

Stephen Fairbank.—Oh, we can easily put that right. It was a sort of practical joke to pay him off for his extempore burst of the morning. The discussion is by no means closed, and I fear we have fired off most of our best charges already. The authors of that book remind me of the makers of dynamite and other terrible explosives. They treat with unconcern matters which in other hands would most probably prove deadly. And I don't feel quite at ease about some of the arguments I took from them this morning. They may be polished up in the Doctor's fertile brain and retorted on us to-morrow in a form not very easy to meet.

Frederick Fairbank.—Which will serve you both right. You *named* Hume and Paley when you quoted them :—but you left Stoffkraft to infer that the *Unseen Universe* arguments were your own. He has evidently been led to over-estimate your powers both of attack and of defence. You are just like a new bowler; while your style is a secret, you are deadly :— presently they will hit you all about :—and then, where are you?

Miss Fairbank.—Right, Fred! I am happy to agree with you.

The Rev. Ralph Bemerton.—Wait till to-morrow before coming to such positive conclusions. Perhaps you may find yourself glad to use *any* argument against the Doctor! I should say, of course, against the Doctor's creed, for the man himself is unexceptionable. You have not yet heard what he thinks of the matters in dispute from the moral and social point of view.

Miss Fairbank.—There I am not afraid of him. These are questions of conscience, and no one with an unperverted conscience could go wrong in such things. Far feebler bonds are effective. Could a well-bred person be guilty of a breach of etiquette?

Elijah Holdfast.—Well said, indeed; but the Doctor is a tough opponent, and I fancy we shall have to do all we know to-morrow.

Sir Kenneth M'Kelpie.—He has two grand defects;—each separately fatal to his authority. He all but denies the existence of the Supernatural, and he looks upon conscience as a weakness;—an amiable one, no doubt, but still unworthy of his ideal.

Miss Fairbank.—I do not think so hardly

of him, Sir Kenneth, he seems to me to be remarkably genial and considerate.

Sir Kenneth M'Kelpie.—Mere habit or disposition :—ineradicable, but sneered at by its possessor, who would have preferred that chance had either made him master of his conscience, or given him none. I tried him with the story of 'Neil the Ranter,' and his comments (for he is a simple, truthful, soul) enabled me to read him thoroughly.

Miss Fairbank.—Is that your usual test, Sir Kenneth? I hope my remarks, when you told it me the other morning, did not reveal any dreadful state of mind?

Sir Kenneth M'Kelpie.—It is a true touchstone, and I never found it fail. But I'll say no more about it to-night. There is a time for everything, and your probable future is not to be discussed now.

Miss Fairbank.—But you'll tell me some day?

Sir Kenneth M'Kelpie.—That I will, and something more—which I have quite recently read :—in the Stars!

CHAPTER V.

THE CONFERENCE IN THE YEW TREE AVENUE.

The palace in a woody vale they found
High raised of stone; a shaded space around:
Where mountain wolves, and brindled lions roam,
(By magic tamed) familiar to the dome.
. . . . . . :
Now on the threshold of the dome they stood,
And heard a voice resounding through the wood
Placed at her loom within, the goddess sung;
The vaulted roofs and solid pavement rung.
. . . . . .
The goddess rising, asks her guests to stay,
Who blindly follow where she leads the way.
. . . . . .
On thrones around with downy coverings graced,
With semblance fair, th' unhappy men she placed.
Milk newly press'd, the sacred flour of wheat,
And honey fresh and Pramnian wines the treat:
But venom'd was the bread, and mix'd the bowl,
With drugs of force to darken all the soul.

THE ODYSSEY, *translated by Pope.*

THE verses we have quoted are admirably descriptive of that Kirkéan monster, a false Philosophy.

Many are the guests whom this infamous enchantress has consigned to the same unutterable doom which overtook the followers of Ulysses, and from which their leader was rescued only by the virtues of the god-given moly.

A change, however, has recently taken place in the policy of the goddess. Some time since her more astute advisers (remembering the wisdom of the serpent—'Eritis sicut Deus, scientes bonum et malum') ventured to remind her that the unvarying sequel to her banquets had already brought her into disrepute, and they suggested as a remedy that she also should have her store of moly—grow it in her kitchen garden, and serve it up at her feasts in such a way that her guests might eat of it or not at their pleasure.

Should any fail to partake of it (they went on to observe) their unutterable doom would be attributed no longer to the goddess but to their own perversity, and thus her feasts might even in time become renowned as nice and delicate tests of character, serving to discriminate between the evil and the good.

The goddess gladly took the insidious counsel, and the moly is now a well-known garnishment at all her banquets.

Thus some of her guests manage to escape the unutterable transformation. Most of them, however, rise from table with a stunned and perplexed look, indicative of the struggle within them between the virtues of one thing and the poison of another. Dr. Stoffkraft, having eaten plentifully of the antidote, was not likely to become wholly the prey of the monster; but, poor moth, he had several times smartly singed himself in her deceitful flame.

And with him the awakening from the delusion was ever as rude as it was certain.

A few words from Stephen Fairbank on the previous day had opened his eyes to the absurdity of one at least of the opinions which he had been confidently because rashly parading; and he felt a sickening misgiving that the whole system might similarly crumble.

Thus he was at the moment prepared to

clutch at any support, rather than be deprived at once of all his laboriously-erected castles.

After a sleepless night, he sought the garden about six o'clock. Frederick Fairbank was there before him, and he had a little book in his hand.

Frederick Fairbank.—Well, Doctor, I feel even more strongly this morning than I did yesterday that they did not give you fair play.

Dr. Hermann Stoffkraft.—How do you mean? Their arguments were quite fair; but I must confess they were more to the purpose than I expected from my adversaries.

Frederick Fairbank.—But the arguments they used were *not theirs!*

Dr. Hermann Stoffkraft.—You surprise me very much. I thought I had read almost every work on the subject, or at least that I knew the tenour of every argument that had been brought forward.

Frederick Fairbank.—But of course you never thought of a modern English book on the subject?

Dr. Hermann Stoffkraft.—No, certainly not. Has any Englishman written anything on these matters—from the genuine scientific side I mean?

Frederick Fairbank.—An anonymous lot—evidently scientific men—have lately brought out a work with the very title, *Unseen Universe*, to which my father led you up yesterday. He and Bemerton have been reading and commenting on the book for some time, and for this reason, no doubt, they adroitly brought you to initiate a discussion of this very subject.

Dr. Hermann Stoffkraft.—And have you seen the book?

Frederick Fairbank.—Here it is! I have looked it through as critics do, sufficiently to be able to talk of it, not more. But *you* must read it carefully.

Dr. Hermann Stoffkraft.—Of course I must read it. But this news is so unexpected that I hardly yet fully realise it. Englishmen attempting scientific speculation! What next?

Frederick Fairbank.—Germans ceasing to do so.

Dr. Hermann Stoffkraft.—No, no; I don't seek wit. I am no match for you or any one in that. How can I turn the tables on these conspirators? I have not time to read this work, much less to think it over, before we resume our discussions. I thought I had so fully considered almost every possible aspect of this question that my antagonists could hardly raise any valid argument quite new to me. But yesterday's experience was not merely perplexing in itself, it has left me with the feeling that some other new and unexpected mines may be sprung on me. Can you not give me a rapid sketch of the argument of this book?

Frederick Fairbank.—I don't think I can. But this at least I can do: if you will indicate one by one the arguments you are about to use, I will tell you how they will probably be met, that is, provided the *Unseen Universe* gives the means of meeting them.

Dr. Hermann Stoffkraft.—I thank you; that is lawyer-like,—at least in all respects but one,—for it is friendly.

Frederick Fairbank.—But don't fancy, Doctor, that if I take your side it is necessarily from conviction. I am naturally combative, and I like above all things a fight, but it must be a fair one. And I am a lawyer, and as such quite as ready to fight on one side as on the other, whatever my private opinions. *Hal-o'-the-Wynd*, in fact, as Sir Kenneth is fond of saying. But proceed to your enumeration.

Dr. Hermann Stoffkraft.—Well, it strikes me that I should begin to-day by pointing out that all the arguments they used yesterday in favour of a possible future state hold good for brutes as well as for men, being based upon the common properties of material organisms.

Frederick Fairbank.—There you wouldn't have a chance. The parson would probably remind you, as he has already done, that when you have once realised the probability of a spiritual

Unseen, it is your interest to inquire whether this order of things has vouchsafed you any information, and your bounden duty to receive such with all humility.

He might go on by supposing one of the apostles to have put this question to their Master, in which case the nature of the reply could hardly be doubtful. 'What is that to thee?—follow thou Me,' would effectually stop a repetition of the question.

My father, again, will point to the fact that the main dissimilarity between men and brutes is not in bodily structure or materials (which must necessarily be the same in both, inasmuch as they both live in the same physical universe), but in style of thought. And then he will turn your argument against you by saying that the unseen concomitants of thought, if they could be scientifically perceived, would almost certainly be very different in the two cases. And remember that it is on these unseen concomitants that part of the scientific argument for a future life is based.

Dr. Hermann Stoffkraft.—I see—that is new, and doubtless taken from this book. I must have time to think over the point: so I shall not attempt this part of my proposed line of argument to-day. My next objection is founded upon the mysterious in their religious system —the doctrine of the Trinity, for instance.

Frederick Fairbank.—You cannot attack them there. They would simply reply that any theory of the nature of God, be it even a materialistic one, is necessarily mysterious: so that mystery cannot be brought forward as a reproach. And they would add, as the authors of the *Unseen Universe* have done, that though their speculations cannot, from the very nature of the problem, give any information on such a subject, they yet lead to results connected with the position of Life and Energy in the Cosmos which are at least perfectly consistent with Christian doctrine. They would then point out the impossibility of conceiving of the Universe without this or some similar doctrine implying development through a spiritual Unseen; and

I think it must be allowed, Doctor, that you were not very successful yesterday when you tried to account for the Universe by means of a dead development.[1]

Dr. Hermann Stoffkraft.—I proposed next to attack the notion of a future state from the point of view of the common doctrine of the Eternity of physical Punishment. Have your *Unseen Universe* authors provided a reply to this?

Frederick Fairbank.—Not that I can see. I noticed that they appeared to avoid the question, though they are several times brought to the verge of it, and this leads me to suspect that possibly they are not quite at one upon it, for they have certainly shown sufficient fearlessness of opinion in other matters. Your antagonists will be driven to their own resources for an answer to this objection, and here I will gladly take your part, for I think I am likely to be heartily on your side. In fact, from my

---

[1] Similar ideas were held by a philosopher of the ninth century, the well-known Johannes Scotus—See article 'Erigena' by Professor Adamson, *Encyclopædia Britannica*, ninth edition.—ED.

point of view (not, of course, from yours), I believe that the monstrous misrepresentations of the New Testament *Gehenna* have had more to do with modern Atheism than all other causes put together. But more of this when the time comes.

Dr. Hermann Stoffkraft.—I am very glad. That is the first crumb of comfort you have given me. Well, I have one powerful argument at least, and no concealed armour in the way of it to prevent my thrusting it home!

Frederick Fairbank.—Don't be too sure of that. I cannot fancy that Bemerton's ideas will be found very different from ours on this subject; and therefore he must have some easy way out of the difficulty.

Dr. Hermann Stoffkraft.—You alarm me; but I have other points of attack; for instance, the inspiration of Scripture.

Frederick Fairbank.—A good subject, but dangerous. Take care it does not cut both ways.

Dr. Hermann Stoffkraft.—And the extreme

limitation, both in space and in time, of the miraculous element in Scripture records. How will that do?

Frederick Fairbank.—I think the *Unseen Universe* deals with this question; but whether it does or no Sir Kenneth will be sure to be drawn by the subject. He has been very quiet as yet; but the supernatural in all its forms is perpetually in his mind.

Dr. Hermann Stoffkraft.—I shall be glad to hear his arguments; for he is evidently an able and original man, though perhaps a mystic. Well, I have enough for to-day at least, unless they raise some quite unexpected issue. And now pray excuse me, I must think over what you have said, and there is but half-an-hour to breakfast.

Frederick Fairbank.—Come with me, and take a header in the pool under the linn, Doctor. That will clear your head and arrange your ideas better than all your secret ponderings.

Dr. Hermann Stoffkraft.—Um Himmelswillen nein. My dear sir, I am not yet accustomed to your violent insular doings; what is pleasure or perhaps necessity to you might be death to me. A cold bath, and before breakfast too. I should be mad—never! (*Exit hurriedly.*)

Frederick Fairbank.—Not a bad little man, and knows a great deal, no doubt. But what is the good of it? Reminds one of his own gigantic octopus, whose stomach may be smashed to pieces before its tentacles cease catching food for it. There isn't a single inch of back-bone in his whole system. He fights by rule and method, and mildly remonstrates with you for lungeing in carte while he is parrying in tierce! A year or two at football and cricket would have made something of him. His knowledge would not have been sensibly the less, but he would have been able to use it. And knowledge is not power except to him who can use it.

I wouldn't exchange physique and habits with the Doctor if I got all the learning of Germany into the bargain.

Whereupon Frederick Fairbank, so musing, reached the clear deep pool, took his solitary 'header,' and forthwith made the best of his way home to breakfast.

The Doctor had fully recovered his spirits, and was gaily chatting with all and sundry. Miss Fairbank affected to attribute his last evening's preoccupation partly to the excitement of his lecture, but chiefly to his unwonted walking performance.

Miss Fairbank.—But if, as we all hope you will, you make some stay with us, Doctor, you will find it indispensable to be a good walker. Scarcely a day passes on which even my cousin and I do not walk at least twice as far as you did yesterday.

Dr. Hermann Stoffkraft.—I shall gladly learn under your auspices. I confess that your brother has a little frightened me this morning, so that I feel somewhat disposed to avoid his tuition. He would have me engage at once in all his rough pastimes, including (what I still shudder to think of) his early morning plunge into ice-cold water! I cannot reconcile the athlete and the philosopher. If he had his will of me, I might perhaps complete the tale of my bad habits by becoming a smoker. What with baths and cricket, fishing, shooting, meals, and the newspapers, and (above all) perpetual smoking, one's whole working day would be mortgaged before one entered on its possession, and its owner would pass through it without having any tangible proof that he had lived otherwise than as a highly-trained wild beast.

Sir Kenneth M'Kelpie.—There I cannot agree with you, Doctor. True, it ill befits me now to speak of such things—years have put several of them quite beyond my power—but while I was under sixty I don't think there were many sports in which I should have shunned a trial even against youngsters like Frederick. And I look back to these days with the full consciousness that my intellectual part had always its fair share of employment :—that is of enjoyment. No one, till he tries, has the least idea how immensely more easily, as well as rapidly, his mind works when his body is kept sedulously in what you have called the 'wild-beast' state, than when by ill-regulated diet and neglect of physical exercise the more tangible part of the complex human machine is allowed to become lethargic or dyspeptic. I shall never forget a remark made by a great medical man, whom I accompanied on his tour of inspection through one of our central prisons, 'See, every one here has a tongue like a dog!' Enforced simplicity of diet and enforced exercise had put these men's bodies into the proper 'wild-beast' state. And is it not obvious that their mental condition must have at least equally benefited? It is with individuals as with nations, the effete voluptuaries of Rome, though once the rulers of the world, went down like nine-pins before the vigorous, because unpampered, Goth. A man who forces his intellect while neglecting his body is in my eyes nothing better than a self-made Strassburg goose, whose whole system is drained in order to exaggerate still farther one monstrously hypertrophied organ. No doubt the spiritual part of a man is infinitely superior to the material part—as the seed-corn to the mere clods in which it has to be buried—but if those clods be not sedulously attended to with plough and harrow, nitrates and phosphates, what becomes of your harvest?

Dr. Hermann Stoffkraft.—This then is, I suppose, your modern British upper-class creed, what I am told is called 'Muscular Christianity'?

Elijah Holdfast.—A mere nickname—smart enough, and likely to stick, because there is some little aptness in it—but, like all nicknames, essentially incomplete and one-sided. Sir Kenneth's ideal, to which I entirely subscribe, is a far loftier thing than what is commonly known as Muscular Christianity—which, to my mind at least, seems to be a sort of reproduction of mediæval knight-errantry and chivalry in a modern dress :—with broad-cloth for mail, and the 'noble science' instead of the 'joyous passage of arms.' All may strive after Sir Kenneth's ideal, for, like the Christian life of which it forms a part, it is open to all :—the Spanish steel-coat and the broad-cloth are sacred to the chivalrous order of the Knight and the Squire. The Yeoman may occasionally be admitted to its ranks, but the Villein *never*.

Dr. Hermann Stoffkraft.—My dear sir, I feel that I have indeed much to learn. Within the last twenty-four hours I have been introduced to a region of which I had hitherto only slight and transient glimpses—so transient that I set them down to fancy. I must observe more before I venture to discuss these matters.

Frederick Fairbank—(*Aside to his father*).— I *must* take him in hand : so he must be kept here at all hazards. He's a splendid little fellow! We'll teach him what he never would have learnt had he attended for a lifetime all the *Realschulen, Polytechnica,* and Universities in his own Fatherland.

Stephen Fairbank.—I fear you will not succeed. The Doctor's early training, or rather want of it, has made it almost impossible to reclaim him by *your* methods. No! If he *is* to be reclaimed the work will be done entirely by a woman. Schiller knew his type well when he said—

> 'Ewig aus der Wahrheit Schranken
> Schweift des Mannes wilde Kraft;
> . . . . .
> Gierig greift er in die Ferne, . . . '

And mark how he immediately indicates the remedy:—

> 'Aber mit zauberisch fesselndem Blicke
> Winken die Frauen den Flüchtling zurücke, . . . '

Depend upon it, this will be the issue.

Frederick Fairbank.—I prefer the other version:—

> 'Des Gedankens Sieg entehret
> Der Gefühle Widerstreit.'

CHAPTER VI.

CONCLUSION OF THE DEBATE.

> Atqui sciebat quae sibi barbarus
> Tortor pararet ; non aliter tamen
> Dimovit obstantes propinquos
>   Et populum reditus morantem,
> Quam si clientum longa negotia
> Dijudicata lite relinqueret. . . .
>
> HORACE.

ON that day the company were assembled punctually at eleven, for it was known to all that Miss Fairbank had requested permission to take part in the debate. Frederick, in fact, privately told Dr. Stoffkraft that 'he would catch it this time, and no mistake.' 'It's all very well,' he said, 'arguing with us. We have conventional rules of debate, and so on. But it is a very different thing when the women come in, as you will speedily find to your cost.' But the Doctor was calm and confident, and his whole expression seemed to indicate absolute faith in the security of his position.

Miss Fairbank.—Although I was not present at the discussion of yesterday afternoon, yet I know all about it from Mr. Bemerton. (*Here an almost imperceptible glance was exchanged between Sir Kenneth and the host.*) I am not sure that I can follow the reasoning, but I could not help wondering very much that the fate of an infinitely important and practical system like Christianity should be placed at the disposal of the victor in a species of intellectual tournament. I have heard of savages staking their clothes, their wives and families, and sometimes even their ornaments; but it has been quite a new experience to me to hear of grave Christian men staking their religion.

For my own part, I quite agree with those who hold that the life of Christ and the lives of all the holy men who have followed in His footsteps, are the best proofs of the truth of Christianity;—these are the things that require to be accounted for. But when I learned from Mr. Bemerton the curious, the strange,—I was going to say the grotesque,—intellectual points upon which the possibility of a future state was made to depend, I must confess I felt inclined to hold up my hands in absolute amazement.

Sir Kenneth M'Kelpie.—I hope you will not consider it as an interruption, Miss Fairbank, if I tell you that all of us (and I don't think I need except Dr. Stoffkraft) will readily admit the superiority of the internal evidence of the truth of Christianity.

But you must remember that very many other things besides Christianity wear two greatly different aspects, according as we view them morally or physically. Let us, for instance, imagine that a great and good monarch lies almost at the point of death. Vast moral and social issues are trembling in the balance, and his death will be felt as a blow to freedom over Europe, and perhaps over the world. This is the moral side of the picture.

Now for the physical side. The patient lies, let us imaginé, in a deep sleep, and if this continues he will do well. The physical requisites for the salvation of Europe are that Carlo should not bark, nor the nurse cough, nor the timbers creak too loudly, for if they do so the King will surely die. Indeed the moral and the physical are very intimately interwoven in this world of ours, and we must just take things as we find them. There are large classes of intelligent men upon whom no impression can be produced by moral reasoning. They pride themselves on being above such a vulgar thing as emotion, and sneer at all religion as being essentially emotional. To them no argument but the physical one is of any consequence.

Miss Fairbank.—It may be so;—indeed I do not think that women can compete with men in strictly intellectual matters, but in morals it is different, and I maintain that the moral instinct of woman is finer as well as more certain than that of man. Now, Dr. Stoffkraft, I have a word to say to you.

K

Dr. Hermann Stoffkraft.—A thousand if you please, for I am sure that every one of them will be kind and good.

Miss Fairbank.—On referring to my notes, I find that the Doctor used the following words in his opening address :—

' Nothing is more painfully ludicrous to me than the way in which men, even of considerable ability, are certain to fall into what average common sense perceives to be the most palpable absurdities, as soon as they begin to lay down principles in political economy, ethics, or metaphysics. Hence probably the reason why (for nearly a century) these subjects have failed to enlist the highest class of thinkers.'

Now I think it likely that Dr. Stoffkraft will assent in a great measure, if not entirely, to that collection of moral principles called the Decalogue. He will likewise own that it is very old,—three thousand years old or more,—and from his point of view he is compelled to believe that it is a veritable product of the moral faculties of man. Thus great advances

CONCLUSION OF THE DEBATE

were made in ethics at a time when physical science was in the most rudimentary state, if indeed it could be said to exist at all.

No doubt, too, the Doctor will view our Saviour as a mere man; but if so, he must be regarded as doing for ethics incomparably more than even Newton did for physics. So completely did Christ grasp the fundamental principles of ethics, that ever since His day the science has been mainly deductive and very much confined to a practical application of the great maxims which were given to the world more than eighteen centuries ago.

On the other hand, physical science has been until very recently in an extremely backward state, and is not this the reason why the strongest intellects have been required to push it rapidly forward? The Doctor would lead us to believe that ethical science is incapable of marching, and that physical science must march on without her; while the truth is, that ethical science is already for ever completed, so far as her general outline and main principles are concerned, and has been as it were waiting for physical science to come up with her. This, from the very nature of things, will never happen.

Dr. Hermann Stoffkraft.—You have quite correctly quoted my words, which, however (so far, at least, as you have called them in question), were intended by me to refer not so much to moral maxims, with the truth of which I quite agree, as to the foundation of our moral convictions, about which (you will bear me out) there has recently been very much controversy.

Miss Fairbank.—No doubt; but if I am not mistaken, there has been an equally animated discussion about the nature of our intellectual acquirements, and whether we have after all any *real* knowledge of outward things.

And you will own that you are not now comparing together our positive acquirements in ethics and physics, but are rather engaged in a semi-metaphysical discussion regarding the foundations of our faculties.

It seems that you have only quite recently

got hold of the conviction, that the intellect must not be put to permanent confusion—in such a way at least as to be able to apply the principle as a weapon. But for a long time a similar principle has been held in ethics and religion, and has also been very extensively applied in practice—it is certainly as old as the Psalmist. Indeed, it is by applying this very principle that I am furnished with what I consider the most powerful argument for a future state, for to deny the existence of such a state would lead, I maintain, to irretrievable moral and spiritual confusion. And now, to conclude, I would ask you all if there be not at the present day too formal a separation between intellectual and religious pursuits, so that while the man and not the woman is chiefly devoted to intellectual matters, the woman and not the man is left to fulfil the duties of religion. Thus the great intellectual arenas are chiefly occupied by the one sex, and the churches very much by the other.

Now, I do not profess to be a strong-minded

woman, or to come prepared with a remedy for all this, but I am not the less certain that it is wrong to separate the two things in this way. It brings about the grotesque result that the man conceives he has an intellectual argument against immortality, into which the woman does not enter, while, on the other hand, the woman conceives she has a moral argument in favour of immortality, into which the man does not enter.

Dr. Hermann Stoffkraft.—What you have just said can be very easily answered—at least I think so. What do you fancy is the reason for the extraordinary excess of feminine over male believers in Christianity? It is not (at least I can honestly say not to my knowledge) any inferiority in point of logical acuteness of intellect. I rather attribute it to what may be called a want of strength of mind—a disposition common to the whole female sex to receive, without questioning, whatever is strongly urged upon their belief. It was Eve, according to the old but well-constructed tale, who was deluded by the serpent—not Adam. And it is the 'silly women' who are led captive according to Paul. So when some fire-breathing ranter abuses his position by gloating over the imagined future agonies of all who differ from him in opinion, however slightly, women listen with wonder and awe, nothing questioning; but the stronger common sense of man requires proof instead of assertion. And here in fact is the strongest of all arguments against the truth of Christianity, and the immortality which it proclaims. In the older creeds the notion of a future state was shadowy and intangible, but doleful alike for good and bad. Mohammed also was consistent—for his Paradise and his Hell were alike sensuous. But if the opinion of the great majority of Christians is to be trusted, their Hell alone is real, sensuous, material; their Heaven altogether vague, mysterious, and intangible. They know every detail about the future condition of the wicked —a condition which is to continue for ever, gradually becoming worse. But the immortality of the righteous is something *per se*, incapable of being conceived, and therefore not to be described by analogy. This won't do. Science and common sense alike proclaim the inherent falsehood of a creed like this. There can be no generic difference of the kind. The best of men cannot possibly be as superior to the least bad, as the least bad is to the worst. In fact, the idea of eternal physical punishment is a purely human one, originally devised to give the more astute of men a fearful hold on the imaginations of their weaker brethren, and still worked with great success in this very way. And a religion which represents its God—the supposed Author of all our ideas of moral right, as condemning to infinitely protracted torture mere finite and exceedingly imperfect beings, is an inhuman, a blasphemous, and therefore a false religion.

Frederick Fairbank.—I am glad to have the opportunity of protesting against what I conceive to be a gross and abominable perversion of truth. I grant at once that if the views stated by Dr. Stoffkraft, and undoubtedly held by many Christians, were at all correct, his conclusion would be inevitable. This is not the time to enter into an argument on the subject, still less to justify my opinion, as I could easily do by references to all parts of Scripture. I will merely say that I cannot imagine how any one can doubt that immortality is there stated to be a boon specially conferred, and on those alone who are accounted worthy.[1] I don't know what Mr. Bemerton may think, but in my opinion this is indubitably the formal doctrine of the Church of England. In the very first Collect of the Christian year we have the petition that in the last day . . . *we may rise to the life immortal.* In the second we pray that *we may embrace and ever hold fast the blessed hope of everlasting life* given to us in Christ. And in another which soon follows, we pray that the Church, enlightened by doctrine, may so walk *that it may at length attain to the light of everlasting life.* In another, that the

---

[1] See *Life in Christ*, by Edward White.

people of God *may be governed and preserved evermore, both in body and soul.* But I need not quote farther examples.

Eschatology must, from the very nature of the case, be one of the most difficult of subjects to the human intellect. But there is a broad general principle which I have always maintained, though I do not recollect having seen it in print, viz., that just as 'a revelation of anything we could find out for ourselves would be an absurdity,' so any ideas we may form (independent of revelation) on a subject where revelation has been vouchsafed to us, *are necessarily absurd.* And thus Mohammed's material Hell completely disposes of the wonderfully similar notions originating in a corrupt state of the Church, and still entertained by many sects of Christians.

The Rev. Ralph Bemerton.—I am afraid I do not quite see the drift of this last point in Frederick's argument. Inspiration, as I take it, is intended to procure us knowledge essential to our well-being, which could not be otherwise obtained. But knowledge is one thing and conjecture another; and conjectures regarding a future state may very well have arisen in the human mind quite independently of revelation, which would then come in either to verify or disprove such conjectures. Thus I imagine inspiration may verify as well as originate.

No doubt the antients had some vague belief in a future state, but they did not regard it as one in which the deeds done in the body were to receive their just retribution. This is clearly shown by the authors of *The Unseen Universe,* who remark that 'while we of the present day regard the future life as in some sense the reward of piety and goodness, the antients looked upon Hades rather as a penalty which inexorable fate had reserved for all men, and from which even piety and goodness were powerless to exempt their possessors.'

One great object of Christ in His utterances was to bring out this aspect of the question, which had somehow fallen into the shade, and He does so by giving a most vivid description of the joys of the righteous and the punishment of the wicked.

He was not addressing a coterie of metaphysical philosophers, and therefore I take it we cannot frame from His words any scientific theory either of the nature of future punishment or of its duration. All that we can gather is (to adopt the words of Dr. Irons), that retribution will be morally complete. We ought to remember that rude Galilean peasants had no true conception of what we mean by eternity, and were likewise quite incapable of grasping the scientific definition of annihilation. Had Christ chosen to inform them that they had lived through a previous existence which they did not now remember, or that in a future state they would forget this present life altogether, they would unquestionably have received His doctrine without hesitation or comment. Indeed, I have myself heard men pretending to believe in a future state deny to the departed any remembrance of their earthly life—men who considered themselves strictly orthodox, but who had evidently a better acquaintance with Christianity than with logic. Therefore I maintain that we are not to look to Christ's sayings for a revelation of the scientific conditions of a future state. Indeed, such a revelation would have been uncalled for. But, on the other hand, Christ gathered together from all quarters every illustration that could lend power to his language, when He described the future state as one of rewards and punishments. The righteous were to enjoy a blissful and honourable existence indefinitely prolonged, while the wicked were to receive punishment and disgrace of indefinite duration likewise. Amongst the various figures of speech which He selected for this purpose, there were two that would tell very powerfully upon the Jewish mind. To the devout Jew the services of the Temple were the very incarnation of holy and honourable enjoyment, and were accordingly borrowed by our Saviour and His apostles in their description of heaven. The Gehenna outside Jerusalem was, on the other hand, the very incarnation of all that was vile and worthless. It was a place where garbage was consumed, where the worm died not, and where the fire was not quenched, and was therefore chosen as a type of the place of the lost. In course of time, however, Jerusalem was destroyed; a race of Christians grew up who knew neither the Temple nor the Gehenna, and these, while they retained, of course, the Saviour's words describing the joys of heaven, were evidently at a loss to discern their true meaning. A vague conception of an ethereal state of endless praise was the result—the eternity of the tabor, as it has been termed by a modern writer. Now such a heaven would certainly not attract the great multitude of mankind, and hence (unconsciously perhaps) theologians and religious teachers felt it incumbent on them, if they could not persuade men out of wickedness by the joys of heaven, to terrify them out of it by the fears of hell, and thus Gehenna came in course of time to give place to a walled-in region of endless physical torment. The impenitent man in the picture of Christ was like a traveller determined to go on a fearful journey amid the blackness of darkness, saluted ever and anon by the muttering of distant thunder and the momentary flash that only served to make darkness visible. To my mind this awful darkness is more impressive not only than the red-light and pasteboard demons of a past age, but even than the sheer fall into nothingness that has recently replaced these antiquated horrors.

Frederick Fairbank.—But do not these awful words, 'Son, remember!' induce us to believe that the remembrance of a neglected and misused past will be one great element in future punishment? There will be a preternaturally vivid remembrance of all that we have done amiss, and in time this will consume our very being, this intensity of remorse gnawing into the very vitals of memory, just as intense pain comes to an end by consuming the organ that gives rise to it.

The Rev. Ralph Bemerton.—I will accept this

as a speculation if you please, but not as a revelation. Perhaps the time may come for such speculations. My conviction is, that just as physical and natural science are gradually improving our knowledge of the origin and progress of cosmical and terrestrial phenomena, the genesis of worlds, and the development of animals, the materials having been all ready before man was created, but being only now made use of—so the true nature of the Christian revelation, for the discovery of which the materials have been in our hands, in a more or less complete form, for eighteen centuries, is becoming more and more clear to those who by freedom from preconceived opinions and by philological knowledge are best fitted for the task. Can we expect that human beings, differing as they do, in the widest manner, on the so-called 'questions of the day,' the materials for judgment on which are in the hands of all, should, all at once, or even in thousands of years, exactly comprehend all that was involved in the Advent, the Life, and the Death of the Author of Christianity? Does religion belong to so different an order of our faculties that we have any *right* to expect that we should now, even after eighteen centuries of patient examination, know all or even much about it? Is it so much more evident than the cause of gravitation, or that of the periodicity of sun-spots and of Eastern famines? Yet these are matters on which we have the means of *fully* judging—give us time enough. Human intellects are very limited, and we must be content to take a great deal on the evidence of our faith, as well as on that of our senses, before reason can be expected to come in to the rescue.

Dr. Hermann Stoffkraft (just a little out of temper).—I shall now, if you please, bring forward the whole question of inspiration.

My first position is that the inspiration of the Scriptures is not plenary—they cannot be verbally inspired.

I will not now refer to certain statements which, taken literally, are simply incredible, even allowing the possibility of the miraculous; but I will confine myself to remarking that different versions of the Old Testament differ in their wording, and that the Septuagint translation, which is largely quoted from in the New Testament, differs in many respects from the English Authorised Version.

Some, I am aware, maintain that while the original manuscript was verbally inspired, differences have in course of time crept in through the mistakes of copyists.

But I am forced to regard an inspiration of this nature, unsupplemented by the continued superintendence of copyists and translators, as a perfectly futile proceeding, leading to no practical result. My next position is, that Christ and his Apostles, as well as the whole Jewish Church at the time of Christ, including the whole of the New Testament writers, believed in the verbal inspiration of the Scriptures. It must be so if we are to judge from their quotations and the way in which they discussed the words of Scripture. There can be no doubt that those upon whom we depend for the Christian religion, including, I venture to say, the Master himself, held an untenable theory in religious matters, and I fail to see how we can reconcile this with the Divine perfection of Christ.

The Rev. Ralph Bemerton.—I believe I am at one with the Doctor regarding the first position which he has assumed. Like him, I do not believe in the plenary verbal inspiration of the Bible, and the Church to which I belong goes no further than to assert that the Scriptures contain the word of God.

I quite think, too, that the plenary and verbal inspiration of the original document, without the continued Divine superintendence of copyists and translators, would be a perfectly futile proceeding. We may therefore dismiss such a hypothesis from our consideration. On the other hand, a verbal inspiration, with the superintendence of copyists and translators, would be a method of procedure very much unlike any of the other works of God; and we may be very glad that it does not exist.

Had there been sufficient evidence for such a system, it would very speedily have produced an arrogant and pedantic caste of copyists, translators, and expounders a thousand times worse than the Scribes and Pharisees of old.

Besides which, all independent thought and spiritual freedom would soon have received their death-blow, and the very life and manhood would have been eaten out of the Church. There would seem to be a very profound tendency in the human mind to attribute a quasi-mechanical, or at least easily perceivable, perfection to all the works of God. I need not recall the great mistake of the schoolmen who would insist on the spotless perfection of the sun and the perfect circularity of the planetary orbits. Whereas the non-circularity of these orbits, when once fully recognised, led Newton onwards and upwards to the great law of universal gravitation; and the study of sun-spots seems destined to lead to equally important results.

Now, applying the same mode of reasoning to the subject before us, may we not hope to glean something from this very want of mechanical perfection in the phraseology of the Bible, and be ultimately led to a higher view of what the Bible really is, and of the way in which we are to learn from it?

Dr. Hermann Stoffkraft.—But, meanwhile, what are we to do? How can we receive the Bible as our rule of faith and practice? Paul himself says:—'If the trumpet give an uncertain sound, who shall prepare himself to the battle?'

The Rev. Ralph Bemerton.—Your objection would be valid if the Bible were to be regarded in the same light as the codified laws of a country, the minutest departure from which will render the transgressor liable to a certain specified penalty; but this is not the case.

The Bible is in great part a venerable and complex historical document, describing the dealings of God with man. It is composed of nearly seventy books, written during the lapse of sixteen hundred years. Now, a mere code of laws may be so explicit as to direct the man who has no moral sense whatever. He may not perceive the beauty of the code; he may even loathe and abhor it; but he can appretiate the sting of the lash, or the hard work and sharp discipline of a jail. But God has intended the Bible to be of use to those who do not smother their heaven-implanted spiritual instinct, even although this may be in a very rudimentary state. To one who has smothered it the letter killeth; but to one who has nursed and tended it, the Spirit giveth life. 'Thy word,' says the Psalmist, 'is a light unto my feet and a lamp unto my path,' but it will not be so to him who has made himself spiritually blind.

Again, revelation is like a tree bearing precious fruit that is good for food. But if a man be so completely disorganised as to be unable to appretiate the fruit, or if he be in doubt whether he should partake of the fruit rather than of the leaves and bark (his senses failing to distinguish between these three things), then it is not probable that he will derive benefit from the tree.

There is an instinct which underlies all our practical operations, and which is independent of our scientific attainments, which it invariably precedes.

A man who has eyes will not decline to make use of light until he is conversant with the undulatory theory, nor will a man who is hungry object to an apple or a piece of bread until he is absolutely master of its chemical constitution.

In like manner we may derive unspeakable practical benefits from the Bible long before we are prepared with a complete theory of inspiration.

It is so in all the arts of life;—we have first of all a rough method of using the materials provided for us, and we ultimately arrive at a knowledge of the scientific principles underlying our method, and are thus able to improve it. The art calls up the science, and the science improves the art.

So with the subject we are discussing. It is intensely interesting as well as instructive to study the Bible scientifically, and try to understand the exact nature of its inspiration; but we may derive the benefits which the book is so well fitted to impart long before our theory is complete.

The upholder of verbal inspiration may perhaps liken the Bible to a tree bearing precious fruit, but he insists that every leaf, nay, every particle, of this tree shall be alive. Well, the critic takes him at his word, and approaching the tree, discovers a dead leaf: on the strength of this, he at once condemns the whole tree. Thus the one extreme calls forth and justifies the other; and, meanwhile, the contending parties are too busy quarrelling with each other to partake of the fruit, which is hanging in rich clusters above their heads. For Death may be found even beneath the shadow of the tree of life.

No doubt the theory of verbal inspiration is a natural consequence of the too general system of breaking up the Scripture record into a vast number of small fragments, each of which is made to furnish an appropriate motto or text for a discourse. A modern writer on this subject speaks as follows :—[1]

'If the Bible be, as we suppose, a record of progressive and continuous revelation, it will carry with it traces of the action of the same intelligence which reveals itself in Nature. What do we find *there?* Nature is a living and complex whole, absolutely unintelligible in fragments, and requiring alike for its scientific explanation and highest practical use connected study of its unity. No man in his senses would now think of treating any science after the fashion in which many of us treat the Divine Revelation, by means exclusively of orations on isolated facts and phenomena.'

And the same writer tells us that 'the Bible as

---

[1] *On Connected Explanation of Holy Scripture*, by the Rev. Edward White.

a whole is an overpowering reply to all important objections to the Bible in detail.' It seems to me quite certain that Christ and his apostles viewed the Bible in this light; they regarded it as a record of progressive and continuous revelation which was to culminate with Christianity, thus forming a species of spiritual evolution. And indeed Christ himself acknowledged certain imperfections in the earlier revelation which were rendered unavoidable by the rude state at that time of the chosen people. While, again, St. Paul gives us, in words that are strangely overlooked, his idea of inspiration, when he tells us 'all scripture is given by inspiration of God, and is profitable for doctrine, for reproof, for correction, for instruction in righteousness.'

God reveals Divine truth in the Bible just as He does corn in the ear. He does not reveal to us, however, the scientific constitution either of the ear of corn, or of the Bible— these we must find out for ourselves. To imagine that Christ, who spoke the words of

Him that sent Him, was commissioned to impart such knowledge, is surely a mistake. Had the gospels contained a long and learned discourse of Christ upon the Elohistic and the Jehovistic records, or upon the authorship of the various books of the Bible, all critics, and you, my dear Doctor, amongst them, would have justly looked upon these documents with profound suspicion.

Dr. Hermann Stoffkraft.—If it would not unduly lengthen out our discussion I should be glad to introduce now the subject of the miraculous. My first remark will be upon certain Old Testament miracles, which are very unlike those said to have been wrought by Christ. In some of these there is conspicuously present the element of violence, with an utter disregard of human life; while in others there is an obvious puerility which (to my mind) at once disposes of their supernatural origin. My next remark is that miracles, if there ever were any, have now ceased for eighteen hundred years. And all the alleged miracles on record are said to have happened in an age which was pre-scientific, and which could not therefore thoroughly examine their claims to be supernatural, inasmuch as man's knowledge of the ordinary course of nature was then very small—so small indeed that many of our modern physical experiments, which even the vulgar see without astonishment, would certainly have appeared miraculous to the most learned of those days.

Sir Kenneth M'Kelpie.—For all that, the events described, if truly described, are as miraculous to our modern knowledge as they could have been to antient ignorance. This is a very strong point as characterising the Scripture miracles. Pardon the digression. I merely wish to ask Dr. Stoffkraft if nature does not sometimes act in a way that seems to be utterly regardless of life.

Dr. Hermann Stoffkraft.—Undoubtedly; and we know how strongly John Stuart Mill felt this difficulty when he said, 'Optimists, in their attempt to prove that "whatever is, is right," are obliged to maintain, not that nature never turns one step from her path to avoid trampling us into destruction, but that it would be very unreasonable in us to expect that she should.

'Pope's "shall gravitation cease when you go by?" may be a just rebuke to any one who should be so silly as to expect common human morality from nature. But if the question were between two men, instead of between a man and a natural phenomenon, that triumphant apostrophe would be thought a rare piece of impudence.'

Now does not all this go to support the position which I assumed at the outset when I supposed myself unable to reconcile the facts of the world with the Infinite power and goodness of God?

Sir Kenneth M‘Kelpie.—I maintain that this question depends altogether on the platform on which we stand; as a little reflection cannot fail to convince us. If there were no hereafter, or even if we were sure that the present life is the end of our spiritual education, and that we crystallise at death, then I grant you we could with difficulty understand the providential dealings of God in permitting the individual to perish through the operation of blind physical laws, and to lose either his being or his chance of salvation. I say, 'with difficulty,' because I do not think I am entitled to use a stronger word. But if we believe in a future state, and imagine that our spiritual education is not ended here, then death is stripped of many of its terrors.

To us, doubtless, who are in the world death will always be a perplexing occurrence, putting human relations out of joint. But to the Governor whose sway embraces both worlds it may wear a very different aspect, and disease and accident may be looked on as His messengers whom he employs to summon his subjects into His presence.

When I see a rock fall and crush to death a fellow-man I associate the occurrence with gloom and wretchedness, simply because I cannot see within the veil. Nevertheless it may wear a very different aspect to the eye of Omniscience. Just as, to our eyes, a caterpillar, a chrysalis, and a butterfly are successive forms of the same individual insect (though, of course, we do not ourselves understand the processes of transformation), while it is pretty certain that a caterpillar would not recognise a butterfly, still less a chrysalis, as something at all of the same kind as itself. It seems to me that the antients read this extremely instructive analogy in a much clearer manner than any one has done in modern times.

Now if the natural occurrences of life are thus ministers which God employs for calling His creatures before him, is there any reason why He should not employ miracles for the same purpose? But if I remember rightly Butler has already handled this subject.

To my mind the true solution is found by supposing that in reality, and to the eye of God, death may be regarded as a comparatively small event in the history of the individual, or at least as not possessing that infinite importance which many assign to it. And any school which maintains an opposite hypothesis must surely manufacture for itself altogether unnecessary difficulties in the way of its grasping the character of God. Nevertheless there is a class of men who do not scruple to hold simultaneously beliefs somewhat like the following.

In the first place, they regard the transition from spiritual death to life, from danger to safety, as a very abrupt one, feebly shadowed forth even by the escape of Noah from the Deluge.

Secondly, they maintain that this transition must take place before physical death, if it is to take place at all.

Thirdly, they frankly acknowledge the absolute recklessness of natural forces that destroy without distinction the evil and the good, the converted and the unconverted.

Fourthly, they maintain that it is presumption to question the justice of God, who is supreme Governor.

Fifthly, they imagine that our own consciences will in a great measure frame our accusation at the great assize.

And lastly, they believe that certain Christians, perhaps they themselves, will take a share as assessors on that occasion.

Now I content myself with the assertion that I cannot see how all these incompatible doctrines can be simultaneously held. Thus the argument must be a very powerful one which would induce me to believe that the spiritual condition of the individual is crystallised at death—whatever the modern hymnist may say :—as, for instance,

> ' Life is the season God hath given
> To fly from hell and rise to heaven.'

But, on the contrary, have we not good reason to think that the primitive church did not hold as a doctrine this hard and fast crystallisation? We all know what St. Peter says about Christ preaching to 'the spirits in prison.' The Church of Rome too believes in a state where souls are purified, and it was only after the Reformation (and because Purgatory had been *utilized*) that the stern (I had almost said savage) theodicy of modern times took its rise.

Dr. Hermann Stoffkraft.—You have said nothing about the puerility of some of the miracles of the Old Testament.

Sir Kenneth M'Kelpie.—Any reasonable communication from the unseen must, in the very nature of things, adapt itself to the state of the human society to which it is made. Possibly some of the miracles of the Old Testament may not commend themselves to Dr. Stoffkraft, a philosopher of the nineteenth century, but they were in perfect accordance with the feelings of the antient Jews. Dr. Stoffkraft believes that this supposed puerility is an infallible proof that these miracles were not of Divine origin, but to my mind the argument goes rather the other way. What are we—the ablest of us—in the sight of Omniscience? In comparison with Omniscience, all human intellects, from that of Newton to the lowest savage or the youngest child, are alike infinitesimal. Besides, even were it not so, a wise father who is anxious to instruct his young child will speak to him in a very different manner from that in which he will address a youth or a grown-up man.

The Rev. Ralph Bemerton.—And when the child has grown up to intellectual adolescence, his father will cease to watch over him with the minute and constant attention he bestowed when he was a child. When the time comes for his being released from leading-strings, he will leave him in a great measure to his own powers, having first done his utmost for his welfare. Now is not this the way in which God has dealt with man? In the fulness of time God sent His own Son into the world, and the character which He manifested, the position which He asserted, and the deeds which He did, combine to furnish a permanent miracle. No doubt it is discriminating in its appeals, but any one who has the slightest inkling of the spiritual sense will not fail to perceive that the Christian idea of Christ is not something that took its rise in the imagination of man. You will perhaps tell me this is no proof of the divinity of Christ; and I will own that we possess no rigorously logical proof. Nevertheless, you have to account for the undoubted fact that a perfect man once lived. Such a fact is simply an astounding moral miracle.[1]

And here, as when dealing with inspiration, let me repeat that our grasp and appretiation of Christianity depend upon the spiritual instinct, and do not pre-suppose a perfect theory either of the inspiration of the Old Testament or of the miraculous element which it contains. The Bible tells us all this very frequently, and in words which I need not now repeat. Rather let me quote from a modern writer, Coleridge, who speaks as follows: 'Whatever may be thought of the genuineness or authority of any part of the book of Daniel, it makes no difference in my belief in Christianity; for Chris-

---

[1] See 'The rationale of Miracles,' *Church Quarterly Review*, April 1876. Also article in the *Saturday Review* upon the same subject.

tianity is within a man, even as he is a being gifted with reason.' And again he says, 'For Christianity proves itself, as the sun is seen by its own light. Its evidence is involved in its existence.'

Sir Kenneth M‘Kelpie.—And that existence is itself a miracle—and a continued one. Men speak of the religious systems of Buddha and of Mohammed as persistent, and therefore possibly genuine. But their persistence is that of everything Eastern—a state of indolent repose, and of *status quo*. How different from an essentially aggressive creed like that of the Christian! What has been considered as Christianity has never for more than a few centuries been *exactly* the same creed—all sorts of so-called Reformations have modified it, and split its adherents into sects innumerable, many of them being in fact almost infinitesimal. But it lives on for all that, and will probably have to suffer many more gigantic Reformations before it becomes anything like the ideal of Christ and His immediate followers. I hope I may call myself a Christian, yet there is no one of the infinitely varied creeds of modern Europe to whose dogmas I can wholly subscribe. What we require is no new Revelation, but simply an adequate conception of the true essence of Christianity. And I believe that, as time goes on, the work of the Holy Spirit will be continuously shown in the gradual insight which the human race will attain into the true essence of the Christian religion. I am thus of opinion that a standing miracle exists, and that it has ever existed:—a direct and continued influence exerted by the supernatural on the natural. I am of course aware of the Scripture which says, 'My spirit shall not always strive with man,' but I interpret it in the sense that ultimately there will be such agreement as to render 'strife' unnecessary, and in fact impossible. But that we are at every instant guided and assisted—morally, perhaps even physically, in our otherwise hopeless struggles, is, I think, all but axiomatic. I would go even further, and say that if it were not so—if the universe and its inhabitants had been, as it were, merely started on a set of rails, already definitely laid down, and had been furnished with the requisite driving power (every precaution being taken to prevent accidents), conscience would have been an absurd and therefore an impossible adjunct, and free will, of which we are all conscious, a violation of natural law. To my mind the whole universe, material or not, is peopled with spirits good or bad. And men's souls live amongst these, just as their bodies do among the conflicting agencies of ozone and disease-germs. While I am on this subject, I should like to tell you of a strange dream I had about a year ago.

Stephen Fairbank.—Let us hear it by all means, Sir Kenneth.

Sir Kenneth M'Kelpie.—I dreamt that a friend and myself were walking one morning under the shadow of the 'Tree of Social Virtues,' and were partaking of its delicious fruit with the most exquisite relish. Now this tree, while its roots are fixed in the Unseen, has thrown out many large branches over the naturalistic paddock, and what was our surprise to find all these swarming with a motley group of men. There were Secularists, Comtists, Atheists, Nihilists, and many more, whose confessions of faith are denoted by words ending in *ist*—they were all there, and each man was provided with a saw. On being hailed, one of their number leered at us over his saw in a most impudent manner, and informed us that he was entitled by law to all the branches that were over his paddock. Each of the *ists* had therefore asked his own surveyor to raise a vertical plane from his boundary line, and to mark the points where this intersected the various branches; and they intended to appropriate these up to the limits of the marks.

But, said my companion, people at your elevation must surely perceive that the roots of the tree are not in your paddock at all.

Hereupon the fellow remarked, with a disgusting gesture, that they were all somewhat shortsighted, and couldn't see so far away as theosophers like us. This of course raised a general laugh at our expense. But what benefit, said I, can you possibly expect from cutting down the branches?

That is our look-out, said the impudent fellow once more: we love this tree just as much as you do, and we know that we are entitled to every leaf of it that lies above our paddock. We mean to have them too; and we have no intention, I can assure you, of poking our heads the least inch beyond the proper boundary. We are great sticklers for law, and will keep to our programme. Hereupon another fellow with appropriate gestures jocularly informed us that they meant to pelt us with the branches of the tree if we didn't leave them alone. This roused my anger against the man, and I shook my cudgel at him, but my friend pulled me back by my skirts. Better leave them alone, said he—let them carry out their programme; come away for half an hour, and they will set to work. When we returned, each man seemed very busy with his saw, and my friend whispered in my ear, 'You see that in order to carry out his programme, each man is obliged to sit on the branch that he is sawing off!!!'

It is a year since I dreamt the dream, but I can remember at this moment the absolutely fiendish glee with which I realised the situation and waited for the coming catastrophe. But there was no such good luck in store, for, of course, I awoke before the event took place.

Dr. Hermann Stoffkraft.—A very remarkable dream, and a solemn warning to all naturalists. I hope I didn't fall very far. I was just about to ask how Sir Kenneth reconciles these remarks of his with the well-known cessation of the miraculous for eighteen centuries.

Sir Kenneth M'Kelpie.—I do so by denying altogether the fact of this cessation. Occurrences have I believe taken place in all ages which are evidently so many signals from the Unseen demanding the surrender of the intellect of man. But alas! many of the 'leaders of thought' are one-eyed men who have lost their spiritual optic altogether. Now mark what they do when this signal is held out. Like Nelson they apply their blind eye to the telescope, and then exclaim 'I can see nothing.' There is a deplorable want of receptivity in such men. When these so-called men of science encounter a rare phenomenon they are ready to receive it on the slightest foundation, if only it chimes in with their preconceived opinions; but if it go against their prejudices they at once dismiss it, with the remark that such an unlikely occurrence demands a practically infinite number of repetitions before they will believe it. Thus they manipulate the evidence to suit their opinions, and not their opinions to agree with the evidence. Now let me give you a short catalogue of various strange phenomena, for each and all of which there is abundant evidence to any one who will keep his eyes open—both eyes remember.

In the first place, there have been frequent and unquestionable apparitions of the spirits of the departed. I will instance only the well-known case in which a murder in New South Wales came to light through the intervention of such a messenger, whose appearance was sworn to before a court of justice.

Secondly, we have mysterious warnings from another world; indeed there are numerous well-authenticated cases in which life has been saved by means of such interventions.

Thirdly, We have the appearance of a distant friend at the moment of his death. I have myself, when in India, experienced a case of this kind, which I thoroughly investigated, noting down the facts without delay; and I found the coincidence in point of time to be exact, and in point of detail complete.

Fourthly, There can be no reasonable doubt of the existence of second sight or clairvoyance. Let me here quote the well-known instance of Swedenborg, who saw by this means the progress of a great fire in a distant city, and told even the very house at which it was arrested.

Fifthly, We have occasionally a supernatural

gift of deriving information, or rather perhaps of divining what is in the mind of another. I think I told you that once at a séance I asked the medium where and when my father had died, and he answered me with the exact expression which I should myself have used in reply; but a year afterwards I discovered that he and I alike had made a mistake.

Sixthly, We have table-turning, levitation, and other allied phenomena, for the truth of which the evidence is very strong, although I grant that such things have been much abused by impostors. I may state that I myself know a little girl, a friend of mine, of undoubted respectability, who, much against her will, is the medium of mysterious rappings, which I have listened to again and again, and tried in vain to account for.

Seventhly, There are, I conceive, well-authenticated instances of what may be called the materialisation of spiritual presences, and indeed I am not without hope that such presences will ultimately, when psychology is better understood, exhibit themselves on public platforms in the light of day.

Elijah Holdfast (sarcastically).—On the floor of the House of Commons, for instance.

Sir Kenneth M'Kelpie (continuing).—Perhaps even there; although the Speaker's eye, Elijah Holdfast's eloquence, and the Usher's black rod would be a combination sufficient to appal the stoutest spirit. And now I will only detain you by adding one more item to my category in the shape of certain miscellaneous occurrences of a mysterious nature. For instance, I do not think the mango-tree performance of Indian jugglers can be accounted for in the same way as the vulgar tricks we see performed by the score. And what do you say to the fact, for it is a fact, that an Indian Fakeer will allow himself to be buried alive for a month or more? Finally, I read of an extraordinary performance which lately took place in Paris before scientific physiologists, in which a girl lay prostrate, having one side of her body quite unconscious, while the other was acutely sensitive to pain; nevertheless, when a magnet was brought near to, but not in contact with, the unconscious side, it suddenly became sensitive, while at the same time the other side was rendered unconscious.

Elijah Holdfast.—Now that Sir Kenneth has exhausted his very singular and interesting catalogue of grotesque mysteries, I venture with all humility to challenge the accuracy of his conception of the supernatural. The buried Fakeer I leave to the physiologists, merely remarking that every hybernating animal does the same thing quite naturally, and therefore, in all likelihood, much better:—and that there is abundant evidence of the existence of a species of catalepsy which is for a time absolutely undistinguishable from death. Possibly accident has led to the discovery of a physical means of producing this state, and the secret is jealously guarded in one particular sect. The question is a very interesting one; but there is certainly nothing of the supernatural in it. I understand by the supernatural such occurrences as tend to exhibit the existence and character of intelligent beings residing in the Unseen. It seems to me quite possible that formal science may ultimately greatly extend its borders; indeed, the theories which try to account for the origin of gravitation and for the production of atoms are attempts in this direction. Should these ultimately succeed, they may possibly throw light on the scientific machinery and capabilities of the Unseen, although I doubt it; but they will throw none upon the character of the Beings which may there reside. The question whether we have had communications from such Beings must be argued by an extension of those habits of thought that lead us to believe there are other human individuals besides ourselves. Now it is well known that in certain diseased states of body or mind we see apparitions. I may, for instance, imagine that a man is sitting opposite me whom nobody else sees. This apparition may affect me injuriously, but it will never give me new information, or assist me in any way.

And this at once disposes of apparitions of all kinds. Nothing can be more vivid than the impression sometimes produced by a dream. Yet when you wake you *know* that the appearances were not objective. So it is with all ghosts; when the credulous or superstitious ghost-seer comes to his senses, he *knows* that he has been deceiving himself. And when we speak of a 'materialised spirit form' we speak of something which, of its very essence, must be, in part at least, natural, and therefore so far capable of being investigated by physical means. Let us have this physical investigation first; and, when that has been satisfactorily carried out, there will certainly remain nothing for farther inquiry, except perhaps by a physician or by a police-magistrate. The Lunatic Asylum or the Pillory (unwisely allowed to become obsolete) would then, in all probability, deserve, if it did not receive, one patient more. The same remark disposes of 'levitation,' 'table-turning,' 'spirit-rapping,' etc. For we all know *respectable* people (to use Sir Kenneth's own word) who lie, cheat, drink, etc., as much as the veriest Bohemian; from whom indeed they differ only for the worse—for your Bohemian is at least honest in not concealing his vices. The one sin these people avoid is swearing—for it is unmistakable, and, to have any effect, it must be done in public.

'Second-sight' presents at first a difficulty, but not, I think, at all an insuperable one. Considering that every really active mind is always at work on speculation of some sort or other, and that we probably hear only of the *one* successful speculation, while the nine hundred and ninety-nine unsuccessful are forgotten almost as soon as conceived, I think that the wonder is rather that the cases of so-called 'second-sight' are so few than that there are any.

What we do hear of are the 'flukes,' and their author is at once credited with consummate skill or supernatural power. It reminds me of Mr. Tupman, when, opening his eyes after firing, he saw a plump partridge in the act of

CONCLUSION OF THE DEBATE.

falling. 'I saw you do it—I observed you pick him out—I noticed you as you raised your piece to take aim; and I will say this, that the best shot in existence could not have done it more beautifully. You are an older hand at this than I thought you, Tupman;—you have been out before.'

Allow for flukes, and you will find that second-sight, dream-revelations, etc., cease to be even remarkable.

Sir Kenneth M'Kelpie.—Mr. Holdfast, you forget that this is not the House of Commons, where members have the privilege of slandering at will all who are non-members without being called to order by the Speaker. You transgress the bounds of courteous debate when you imply that a young girl of nine years, a relative of mine, in whose presence raps are produced, is not merely a conscious deceiver, but has the unparalleled effrontery to pretend that she exceedingly dislikes the part she is forced to play. You may perhaps allege that anything connected with table-rapping must *ipso facto* be considered imposture; but I must, as a gentleman, decline taking part in any discussion where such offensive dogmatism is allowed.

Elijah Holdfast.—I much regret if I have attributed imposture to a—Highland cousin of Sir *K*enneth's.

Sir Kenneth M‘Kelpie.—She is my niece, Sir, and an Englishwoman, but I will let it pass after what you have said. And now I have a word to say about the 'flukes,' as you call them. You know of course that it is possible to calculate probabilities; you can therefore tell me what were the chances that a friend, whom I left in perfect health, should die sometime in 1845, his thirty-sixth year. Besides, the apparition of a distant friend is not a common occurrence, even to a Highlander. I myself never saw another, and it is therefore possible to calculate, roughly at least, the chance of my having seen such an apparition in that particular year. Both events were, taken apart, very unlikely to have happened. How extremely improbable then is it that they should by chance have occurred together, as nearly as possible at the very same moment of time.

Elijah Holdfast.—I will, if you please, Sir Kenneth, leave the calculation of such probabilities to the Doctor, who is a better mathematician than I. But you will allow me to remark that such occurrences, even if true, and remember I don't admit their truth, are not supernatural, because they do not point to the existence of intelligent agencies and powers residing in the Unseen.

Then with regard to the spiritualistic phenomena, the authors of the *Unseen Universe* draw what is, I think, a very just distinction between the miracles of Christianity and the so-called spiritualistic miracles. The miracles of Christianity had an object in view, gave new information, and invaded the world.

The spiritualistic miracles have no object, give no new information, and, far from invading the world, are exhibited only under conditions which are adverse to scientific scrutiny.

I agree with Sir Kenneth about the want of receptivity of the leaders of thought, but he has, I think, overdrawn his simile about the signal held out from the Unseen. The true signal is the Life and Character of Christ, and any one who has spiritual eyesight may see this signal without a telescope. To slight this evidence and go to spiritualism is to be like a man who believes in celestial luminaries, not because the sun enlightens the world, but because with a telescope of sufficient power he is able to detect the satellites of Mars.

Sir Kenneth M‘Kelpie.—Then you will probably not even allow that some of these phenomena point to a constitution of the Universe inconsistent with the materialistic hypothesis of atoms?

Elijah Holdfast.—Not so; though there is but one of them to which I can assign any weight. It is the influence of one will on another and less powerful one. I think it is pretty clearly *proved* that there is a real basis for what has been called Electro-biology; indeed

I think it is the true explanation of all these grotesque phenomena. Much that is absolutely absurd must be cleared away, but still there will, I think, remain a good deal to be accounted for. But if this be granted, to ever so slight an extent, it is a most telling argument against materialism, for it involves necessarily (from the materialist's point of view) a species of distance-action between atoms—the very notion which, as I am told, all the higher science of the day is doing its best to upset.

Dr. Hermann Stoffkraft.—Stay—let me see, or at least it would involve a sensorium in the unseen: which I cannot allow. This is by far the most telling argument I have yet heard, and I confess that (for the moment at least) I do not see how to meet it. If I am right, there must be a weak link in the chain, and it can be no other than the assumption that some at least of the phenomena of Electro-biology are genuine. I must again examine them.

Sir Kenneth M'Kelpie.—An excellent opportunity presents itself, Doctor. Next week I hope to entertain two of your compatriots, who are special adepts in Electro-biology, and are also 'mediums' of some note. Graf Ernst von Ehrenberg and his sister you must at least have heard of.

Dr. Hermann Stoffkraft.—I am happy to call him an intimate friend. We were fellow-students in days when both were impecunious, and when a common patron provided for us at the University. Strange to say, we can still, without shame, acknowledge our obligations to him, great as they are. We were told that the 'correct thing' was to cut him as soon as we could stand on our own feet. But Count Ernst, like myself, is a victim to conscience! His sister, I remember, was a merry little girl some dozen or so years ago. She must be a woman now.

Sir Kenneth M'Kelpie.—And one of the most charming of her sex, as I am sure you will confess when you have met her. But she is altogether above the frivolities of fashion—she has a mission—and, like all such semi-inspired people, she cares not to think or talk of anything else. Come with me to-morrow to Strathkelpie, Doctor, and learn the truth from a woman.

Frederick Fairbank (aside to Dr. Stoffkraft). —Don't be a fool. It's all up with you if you go north. Besides, you have already agreed to stay with us.

Dr. Hermann Stoffkraft (to Stephen Fairbank).—My dear Sir, I feel I must beg you to release me from my engagement with you, and as nothing but my intense desire for knowledge could have induced me to revoke my promise, so I hope you will forgive me.

Stephen Fairbank.—Of course, Doctor. I see how it must all go. Second-sight or not, I divined your fate this morning, as Frederick there will tell you. But I had no idea that it was so imminent.

Sir Kenneth M‘Kelpie.—What is all this? I thought second-sight was peculiar to the Scottish Highlanders. Is Saul also among the prophets? But I think, Fairbank, that the

Doctor should travel with me, as my quarters are not very easily accessible. You can catch him, and detain him as long as you please, on his way home. I'll give you due notice.

Stephen Fairbank.—Be it so. I had much to show him, much to say to him, and still more to learn from him. But I see that his heart is fixed on your spiritualistic work, for the time at least, so we must prorogue the Paradoxical at once, and hope for better success at our next meeting.

Frederick Fairbank (aside).—That's always the way. What's the use of bothering about them? My father has some common sense, and applies it to his beliefs, but Sir Kenneth will believe anything, and Stoffkraft nothing. Yet these two extremes go off together for some outrageous folly, and leave the common-sense mean behind. Well! I have done what I could, short of utter rudeness—so I wash my hands of the whole affair.

CHAPTER VII.

WHAT BECAME OF THE DOCTOR.

> ' Unglücklicher, was willst du thun ? so ruft
> In seinem Innern eine treue Stimme,
> Versuchen den Allheiligen willst du ?
> Kein Sterblicher, sprach des Orakels Mund,
> Rückt diesen Schleier, bis ich selbst ihn hebe.
> Doch setzte nicht derselbe Mund hinzu :
> Wer diesen Schleier hebt, soll Wahrheit schauen ? '
> SCHILLER.

A COUPLE of years have passed since the Jubilee party broke up. During the recent autumn the editors enjoyed for a short time the hospitality of the genial Stephen Fairbank. Trout were plentiful, and gave excellent sport. The morning 'header' was as grateful as ever. Frederick Fairbank, home for the vacation, was busily engaged in training a cricket eleven to do battle with some neighbouring power, and we gave him what help we could. But it was felt by both of us that a great change had taken place in Elmsly House:—all the arrangements were as perfect as ever, yet an indefinite charm which used to pervade the house was wanting—

'Tis Greece, but living Greece no more.'

No Miss Fairbank presided at her father's table. But in the vicarage there was now a Mrs. Bemerton, whose attention was all but entirely concentrated on her husband and her little son; and she was very like Miss Fairbank indeed. She received us with all her old grace and kindness, but it was clear that she had not quite passed through the transition state. The unusually long honeymoon was yet very near the meridian. Mr. Bemerton could with difficulty be induced to leave his wife, even for an hour, and when he did, he could talk of little else.

'*He's* a frightful spoon, and I'm sure my father misses *her* tremendously,' Frederick said to us in his artless manner. 'I know he now wants me to marry and settle down in the country with him. But he won't say so :—his principles before his comfort :—he feels that I ought to work, and he would die rather than breathe a hint of what is uppermost in his mind. But I'm going to reconcile his wishes and his convictions in a way he doesn't expect. I'm going to cut the bar, and take to the counting-house, to which I used to have an insurmountable aversion. I have already secured the promise of a future partner (I don't think she is any stranger to you), who will do the honours as well at least as Mrs. Bemerton.'

Having heartily congratulated him (for we understood at once that he spoke of his charming cousin), we asked about Sir Kenneth, and most particularly about our friend Dr. Hermann Stoffkraft and his fortunes.

Frederick Fairbank.—There's a long and queer story there, and I am not sure that I know all about it. Stoffkraft has given up for good his materialistic notions. Bemerton and my father began the work, but the Gräfin and Sir Kenneth, with the help of Father

Prediger, effectually finished it. The Doctor is a Geheimrath now, and the Gräfin is his wife! What do you say to that? She had enough sense and strength of mind to have thrown caste to the winds, and married the plebeian Doctor, but the Privy Councillorship has luckily prevented the necessity of such a frightful breach of etiquette. But my father will tell you about the business. He has had lots of letters from all of them. Leave that to the evening and come with me:—my eleven will be savage if we don't give them some swift round-hand this afternoon.

There was nothing for it but to accompany the enthusiast, who kept us at work till the first dinner-bell rang.

After dinner, which for once reminded us of old times, because Mr. Bemerton and his wife were present, Stephen Fairbank produced a mass of correspondence, from which he extracted a few characteristic letters sufficiently connected to form a nearly continuous, though of course not exhaustive, narrative.

SIR KENNETH M'KELPIE to STEPHEN FAIRBANK.

'STRATHKELPIE CASTLE, *June* 21*st*, 1876.

'MY DEAR FAIRBANK,—My distinguished German guests have now been with me for ten days, and my young niece, whose fair name was the innocent cause of a passage at arms between Elijah Holdfast and myself, is here likewise—so you see the spiritualistic element is very strong. I gladly comply with your request to give you a long account of our proceedings. As precision of thought is essential, I will divide these into three categories—table-rapping, action at a distance, and materialisation; and I will begin with table-rapping. Here my niece has been a host in herself, albeit an unwilling one; and I can assure you we have all (the Doctor included) tried our best to find out the physical cause of these knocks, but absolutely without success. That they are objective realities, I have not the smallest doubt; for a complete stranger once made his appearance at the open door of the room in which we were sitting, and heard them as well as ourselves. Besides, it is preposterous to suppose that an unwilling girl, only nine years old, should be able to delude a whole company of grown-up people into the conviction that they hear sounds which have no real existence.

'You know of course that these knocks convey a spiritual communication; to compare great things with small, they may be likened to the signals of a telegraphic instrument delivering a message from the Unseen. Sceptics of course deny this, and assert that the message takes its rise from some one of the very prosaic human intelligences gathered together on a fool's errand; but I can assure you that the communications received by us were utterly out of keeping with the habits of thought of any of my guests. On one occasion the *Poltergeist* (for so Dr. Stoffkraft habitually names it) pretended to represent the spirit of a beautiful cousin of mine whom I knew in days long gone by, and who now told us she was married to a North American Indian, and that Bacchus had been best man! And on another occasion our volatile friend rapped out Ta, ta, for the present—I'm off for a ride! Now, my dear Fairbank, what *is* to be made of all this, for we cannot, as members of the Paradoxical, shut our eyes to it?

'I have thought deeply over the subject, and now present you with a preliminary hypothesis. May not these poltergeists be the spirits of those who were the *imps* and *pickles* of this world, but who died in early youth before their education was finished? This will of course go on after death, and in order to complete their character, they may be allowed to have their fun out.

Coelum non animum mutant qui trans mare currunt,

may be true so far as they are concerned, even after crossing the Styx; and the really harmless, yet somewhat unpleasant, boy who used to torment the baby and the dog as a daily rule, but who only on rare occasions had the supreme felicity of practising on a grown-up person, may now with impunity bamboozle the philosopher. Indeed, I think this theory will account for the dreary and confusing character of many of these manifestations. You know there are men of science who assert that they would rather not have the kind of immortality such séances pretend to disclose, and which one of them has comically characterised as

'Rapping idiot thoughts on tables under vulgar cheats' control.'

The poltergeist may, however, regard the whole affair as a huge joke, and be all the while laughing in his sleeve at the credulity of us mortals. So much for table-rapping.

'I now proceed to action at a distance, including its two subdivisions, electro-biology and clairvoyance, in both of which I flatter myself we have succeeded to perfection. And first of all I can dispose of Elijah Holdfast's theory of strength of will, for we found that Ernst could act upon his sister and also his sister on him. And it was very amusing to watch the fair Julia obtain complete command of the poor Doctor, who was persuaded that his walking-stick was an umbrella, and that a glass of water was the best Glenlivet (a great mistake this!). The Doctor, however, had his revenge, and conquered the fair Julia in his turn, persuading her that a piece of glass was a diamond of the first water, and also that he (the Doctor) and the fair Julia were brother and sister. Well! well! Fairbank, we live in a queer world, and I begin to believe there may have been such things as love philtres after all.

'Yesterday afternoon, when the Doctor was practising on Julia, he happened to ask her if she could transport herself to Elmsly House. She immediately described it to perfection, and told us the company were assembled at dinner. She was then asked if she could hear the conversation, and she informed us that a young man, whom she described, was telling a story to a young lady next him. After a while she said the tale is finished, and the young lady has just exclaimed—O Fred, what a funny story!'

Here we ventured to interrupt Stephen Fairbank, who was reading aloud this letter, to ask if the fair Julia had been correct in her divination.

Frederick Fairbank (blushing a little).—Well! yes, correct on the whole, but of course the Doctor knew that I always sat next my cousin, and invariably told her not only one story, but several. He knew, too (the sly old fox) that Fanny used constantly to say—O Fred, what a funny story!—no, no, one swallow does not make a summer.

Stephen Fairbank.—Well, to proceed with Sir Kenneth's letter :—' We next attempted the materialisation of spirits, but here we met with little success. Only on one occasion a form was seen by Ernst and his sister, but it wanted definition, the only parts that were clearly visible being the nose and the right elbow. None of the others perceived it at all. These phenomena, I begin to think, are not objective, but due to a diabolical influence on the mind; and I have no doubt our small success was owing to the conditions of our circle being very unfavourable for such manifestations (I mean, of course, spiritualistically unfavourable). And here I may remark that our ancestors had truer ideas regarding materialisation than is generally held in the advanced circles of the present day, for in Marlowe's *Tragical History of Doctor Faustus*,[1] that worthy, on being asked by the Emperor to bring up before him Alexander the Great and his beauteous paramour, replies as follows: "My gracious lord, I am ready to accomplish your request, so far forth as by art and power of my spirit I am able to perform. But, if it like your Grace, it is not in my ability to present before your eyes the true substantial bodies of those deceased princes, which long since are consumed to dust. But such spirits as can lively resemble Alexander and his paramour shall appear before your Grace, in that manner that they both lived in, in their most flourishing estate; which I doubt not shall sufficiently content your Imperial Majesty."

---

[1] See Marlowe's *Tragical History of Doctor Faustus*. Clarendon Press series. A. W. Ward.

'Well you see I have thoroughly fulfilled my promise, and now you must let me know how things are going on with you since we left. How about Miss Fairbank and the Parson, and Fred and the charming Fanny, are they all well? Give them an old man's love, and believe me, ever yours truly,

'KENNETH M'KELPIE.'

Frederick Fairbank.—I need not tell you how angry we all were on receipt of this letter. We believed the old reprobate had got hold of the Doctor and intended to ruin him, but you will see as we go on that things did not turn out so badly after all.

Stephen Fairbank.—Meanwhile you might like to hear the Doctor's letter, giving *his* views of the experiments.

DR. STOFFKRAFT to STEPHEN FAIRBANK.

'STRATHKELPIE CASTLE, *July 4th*, 1876.

'MY DEAR SIR,—I did indeed promise to write soon and often to you from this northern castle, but I have found so very much to interest me as well scientifically as socially that almost unwittingly I have allowed more than a whole fortnight to pass.

'The weather has been extremely rough since I came here, so much so that we have scarcely seen even the immediate neighbourhood. We have a magnificent view of the Atlantic, and the tremendous swell rolling in after some days of a north-west gale far surpasses in grandeur any natural phenomenon I have yet seen.

'But if it is uncomfortable outside the castle, it is quite the reverse within. I have now been in many a pleasant circle in your hospitable country; but, without any disparagement to the others, this transcends anything I have yet seen. You will say, perhaps, that some of the other guests being from my own country has something to do with it! I cannot allow that. I ask myself what is the reason; and I find it in this, that we spend our days, and evenings alike, in rational discussion and experiment—we have no morning 'headers,' and no day-long athletics. And, at least till the weather improves, we shall not try to get into the 'wild-beast state.'

'You will ask how my inquiry goes on, for the sake of which I so unceremoniously left you. That is not easy to answer.

'On one point alone I see quite clear. The 'respectable' little lady is—well, not an impostor, only an imp. I caught her eye on one occasion after a séance, and it betrayed such a startling mixture of the cherub and the fiend, that I felt quite sure she was the prime mover of the whole performance. For such a *rôle* her age is no objection, but rather the reverse. She was born an imp, and her sense of scientific morality is not yet sufficiently cultivated to overcome the fiendish pleasure she experiences in deluding her uncle. Of course, when she is fifteen or sixteen, we shall hear no more of table-rapping. I have not told Sir Kenneth—remembering how ill he took it when Mr. Holdfast said something not very flattering. But I heard the raps. I proved that they were objective, and by degrees traced them to her foot under the table. Yet her foot when carefully watched did not appear to move. I saw then that the origin of the sound was *inside her shoes*, and after a little practice I found it very easy indeed to produce rapping like hers. To make sure, I privately took a very large and shallow tea tray, and just before the performance inverted it under the carpet, in such a way that when the girl was seated in her usual position her feet must rest on it. The first rap she gave evidently startled her with its loud resonance, and she could (or rather would) do no more that night. I need not say that (before morning) I replaced the tray in its former position. Next night she rapped quite freely after a little nervousness in commencing. Keeping my eye fixed on her, I then began to rap also. She started, looked at me for a moment in a wild way, and hurriedly left the room. I have not heard her perform since. But I cannot bear to tell Sir Kenneth, it would so much distress him, yet he ought to know the truth. What should I do?

'My other inquiries have been more mysterious and much more pleasing. I am quite satisfied that there is something real in Electro-biology; though almost any other name would be better; for it seems to me to have nothing to do with biology, and still less with electricity. That one human being can by merely willing it, and absolutely without any outward sign, affect the thoughts of another, I have as yet no proof. But I now know how *very* little of outward sign is sufficient to telegraph as it were a whole world of meaning! This is in itself extraordinary, and must be eliminated before any satisfactory answer can be obtained to the great question I have before me. I feel quite sure that most, if not all, of what I have yet seen of Electro-biology:— extremely singular as it is—is due to the very slightest of signals by eye, tone, or gesture; and that the spell is *voluntarily* submitted to is I think proved by the fact that any sudden distraction (especially of a nature to provoke resentment) sends it to the winds at once.

'This was most effectually shown the other night when Count Ernst operated on some of Sir Kenneth's keepers and ghillies. He made them go through a number of antics, while they seemed unable to resist, though certainly conscious that they were being laughed at. At last he planted himself full in front of a gigantic Highlander, and defied him to strike him—let him hit as hard as he could. The giant struck with all his might a set of blows, each of which would have felled an ox, but Count Ernst stood calmly within reach, and with a slight gesture of his hand waved aside (*not parried*) the blows as they came. Then he told another of his patients to take his place and stand firm. " I will take care," he said, "that he does not hit you," and, waving as before, placed himself beside the new comer, who stood like a statue. But there must have been some grudge between these two men, or the spell was in some way weakened, for the very first blow went home with a crash, straight on the nose of the too confiding victim, and sent him flying to the other end of the hall! In an instant he was on his feet, and a frightful struggle commenced. But Sir Kenneth, with great promptitude, had them overpowered by numbers and separated. He has had to interpose his patriarchal authority, which is final with these rude people, to prevent serious consequences.

'The clairvoyance I have seen as yet has not much impressed me from the scientific point of view. Perhaps it is true, as I sometimes fancy, that I am too much engaged in looking at the medium herself to pay much attention to her revelations. Nothing has been said that did not appear to me to be quite natural under the circumstances: in fact the medium's words, when I interrogated her, seemed exactly to follow the train of my own thoughts as regards the question asked. Perhaps at another time I should have wondered at this. Not so now. It is strange to me how the last few days seem to have deprived me of my old scientific modes of procedure, how much more I think of persons than of phenomena, and how little my once habitual caution and suspicion make themselves felt. Everything about Sir Kenneth is a mystery, and his castle and its inhabitants are no exception.

'I fear you will think this a very poor letter. But I must frankly confess I am unable to write a better. The weird influence of the place is over me, and I feel as if knowledge were, after all, a vain pursuit—that human happiness in short should be human and not bookish.

'But I tire you, for I do not understand myself.—Yours truly,

HERMANN STOFFKRAFT.'

'*P.S.*—There is a priest here—by name Prediger—who is the 'director' of the Count and his sister. He is a somewhat austere man, but very well informed, and quite as ready as was Mr. Bemerton to discuss matters of science. I feel as if it were not improbable that in a few days we shall be discussing matter and immortality here to the full as extensively as we did at Elmsly House. I may tell you that I have now fully studied the *Unseen Universe*, some parts of it indeed with no little pleasure. I have not yet, however, quite made up my mind on the whole subject—so I shall defer it to another occasion.'

Frederick Fairbank.—There's nothing in his postscript, but I think his letter is singularly expressive. You can read between the lines the writer's quite *naïve* expression of an affection which he is not yet even aware of feeling.

Mrs. Bemerton.—Of course. The moment I saw that letter I knew the little man's case far better than he did himself. Well, he had a terrible time of it, poor fellow—but he is thoroughly happy now.

Stephen Fairbank.—You forget, dear, that our friends are only beginning to learn his story. Here is a second letter from Sir Kenneth, which carries it more than a twelvemonth farther.

SIR KENNETH M'KELPIE to STEPHEN FAIRBANK.

'STRATHKELPIE CASTLE, *March* 5, 1878.

'MY DEAR FAIRBANK,—You know, of course, that our good friend the Doctor has been for some time married to the Countess Julia. Their courtship and all its accessories form a very interesting as well as amusing episode in my life. They looked upon me almost as a father, and told me from day to day all their little joys and sorrows, poor things, so I shall have a great deal of news to give you when we meet. More thoroughly honest, simple, and worthy people I have never met. I need not tell you how happy I was when I first heard of their engagement. The Doctor, you know, had in a very short time after leaving you become an ardent spiritualist, and was under the belief that mediums would form the 'coming race;' and he could not help dwelling with infinite, yet artless, complacency upon the chances in the struggle for place and power which might fall to the lot of the children of such parents. Well! well! Fairbank, all this may sound very strange to moderate men like you or me, but we must not discourage youthful enthusiasm, my friend.

'How happy they both were, and how pleasantly each day flowed on! A large part of it was of course devoted to the courtly observances of the etiquette exacted by their relative position. Even in the midst of these, however, they found time for the pursuit of certain important spiritualistic experiments. But there is no Eden without its serpent, and here the serpent was the Reverend Father Prediger. I am aware that he is a great friend of yours and Frederick's, and I cannot but respect his talents and his character; but, Fairbank, *I hate that man.* Honestly, no doubt, and in strict discharge of what he deemed his duty, he has done irreparable injury to science. You know, of course, that before the jubilee the Doctor was labouring away in the hopeless slough of materialistic mud—well! you and Bemerton placed one stepping-stone for him, and I another; for I must tell you that when he left Strathkelpie he was quite convinced, by our reasonings and by personal experience, of the existence of a spiritual Unseen.

'Shortly afterwards he made a determined spring towards the religious platform, to which, of course, the Reverend Father was only too glad to assist him. But no sooner was he safely landed there than with one vigorous effort the Reverend Father kicked away the spiritualistic stepping-stone. To show you how well the thing was done, let me transcribe part of a letter which I had from the poor Doctor :— " The good Father Prediger is a frequent visitor both to Julia and to me. He is a most amusing and intelligent man. One day lately he was announced when I was on my usual morning visit to Julia, and we were all three speedily engaged in agreeable conversation. Julia happened to suggest that we should tell Father Prediger about our spiritualistic experiments, as perhaps he would like to know something about them. The Father expressed himself very greatly interested, and I gave him a long account of all that we had been doing. In reply he divided the subject into two categories, one consisting of electro-biology and clairvoyance, and the other of table-rappings, materialisations, and such like. 'These last,' said he, 'are, if genuine, probably somehow connected with intelligences residing in the Unseen. It is a subject of great interest and practical importance.' 'I am glad to hear you say so, Father,' I replied, 'for Julia and myself both think so, and we are vastly interested in our experiments.' 'There is one point, however,' continued the Father, 'about which I should like to have a little more information. Have you been able to convince yourselves of the honesty of the spirits, if such they be, who give you these communications?' I replied that we had not thought of the subject in this light. 'Well,' said he, 'had you not better do so at once? For if you believe in the existence of a spiritual Unseen which has any relation to man, *there must be evil in it!* And that evil is perhaps, nay probably, organised. I don't ask you to believe in the mediæval Devil, but common sense requires you to assent to the possibility at least of a powerful unseen federation for evil purposes. Now, directly or indirectly, it does not matter which, and I don't know, I believe the powers of evil are connected with table-rappings and materialisations.' 'But,' said I, 'Father, is it not a point of great interest to know whether these manifestations are objective or only subjective?' 'It is no doubt a point of some interest,' he replied, slightly laughing, 'but yet only of secondary importance. If you and I, Doctor, had missed our way, and strayed into the grounds of some terrific ogre, the discussion as to whether we should more probably be flayed alive or chopped into minced meat, when taken, might perhaps prove interesting, but if the gate were still open, it would be secondary in importance to the act of making our escape.' 'And you would advise us, Father, to give up these spirit-rappings and materialisations?' 'Most decidedly I should,' replied the worthy Father. 'Well, what about electro-biology and clairvoyance?' said I. 'I don't imagine, said he, 'there is anything supernatural in these, so that I cannot object to them as your spiritual adviser; but as a friend—' 'You object to them?' I asked. 'Well,' he replied, 'you and the Countess are about to take a most solemn step, attended with very serious responsibilities, and I much question whether you or she will be able to discharge your duties so well if you give yourselves up to these peculiar manifestations. But I leave this matter entirely to yourselves, and I shall always feel greatly interested in the progress of your experiments.'"

'Thus you see, my dear Fairbank, how the poison was beginning to work; and I will now give you a short extract from a letter which I had from the fair Julia some months after her marriage:—"Father Prediger calls very frequently, and seems much interested in the progress of our experiments on electro-biology and clairvoyance, but Hermann is only half-hearted about them; in fact, he seems inclined to give them up, and to devote his whole time to his old mathematical and physical studies."

'And six months afterwards she writes:—"Hermann has just made himself a great name;

he is universally spoken about, and Father Prediger says he considers him the most distinguished mathematician of the age.

'"He has recently worked up his almost forgotten mathematical MSS., and has published three memoirs which are everywhere discussed in scientific circles. One of these is 'A Complete Theory of Canonizants,' another on 'The Physical Determination of Beknottedness,' and the third 'Ueber Mannigfaltigkeiten in vier Dimensionen,' whose title I cannot express in English. Unfortunately I am totally unable to understand any of them, but no doubt they must be of great scientific importance. I shall have much pleasure in forwarding copies of them to you, or to any of your friends whom they are likely to interest." Now, Fairbank, just think of all this—it is enough to make angels weep. Here is a man of immense ability, who till lately was engaged in the most engrossing and important pursuits, and he is now driven by ghostly influence to leave them for subjects not only utterly pedantic but singularly barren of useful results. Who knows or cares about Canonizants? I must confess I don't. Beknottedness seems but one step from Besottedness, and must mean some species of tangled intellectual trifling, if it have any meaning at all. In his third paper, I am told, the Doctor seriously and at great length discusses the possibility of performing certain unthinkable operations under given inconceivable conditions! And for *this* he is famous! But I must hasten to a close.—Love to the Bemertons, not forgetting Fred and the charming Fanny, and believe me ever yours truly,

'Kenneth M'Kelpie.'

Stephen Fairbank.—One recent letter must be inflicted on you. It is from the Doctor to our friend Holdfast, who forwarded it to me after making all sorts of pencil comments on it, which in themselves almost amount to a letter. He rarely writes in any other way, so you may well fancy I get strange medleys from him. At present he is crazed about politics.

Dr. Hermann Stoffkraft to E. Holdfast, M.P.

'Schloss Ehrenberg, Baden, *Aug.* 12, 1878.

'My dear Mr. Holdfast,—I do not know whether or not the custom obtains in England, but with us in Germany it is thought right for a man to inform all his friends, sometimes almost minutely, of the occurrence of matters of any considerable importance to himself. (*Thank goodness I haven't many German friends.*) I have two reasons, however, for being brief. My friends in England are so numerous that to write a long letter to each would occupy some months, and I cannot send a circular. (*Why not make a pamphlet of it at once, and advertise it? His naïve confessions and confidences would pay.*) And I know that you are always very busy. (*Thanks to Imperialism, Cyprus, and Afghanistan, every one of us has plenty on his mind. But my constituents go in for Jingoism to a man, hang them!*) So I shall confine myself to telling you that the results of my visit to Strathkelpie have been very numerous, and, to me, of immense consequence.

'In spite of the incredulous laughter of the party at Elmsly House, I believed myself destined, as I told them, to become an old bachelor. (*No doubt he did; he was quite truthful, but quite ignorant of himself.*) I am now happily married, and feel myself in all respects improved in consequence. (*He couldn't well help that, unless he had married a fool.*) I have recently reverted to my old mathematical and physical papers, and such of them as I have yet published have been exceedingly well received. (*By whom? I should like to know. Quips, quirks, and conundrums. Call that science!*) Should I desire or require it, I am now certain of a Professor's chair. (*Best thing he could do: give him some work that must be done, and keep his wits from going a wool-gathering.*) I have even been promoted to civil distinction, in a form which enables me to have an influence on public affairs. (*Fancy mathematics making a man a Privy Councillor!*

No doubt literature has something to say for it with us, and if the Tories have a Premier of that kind we have had a couple at least. But mathematics! I always said these Germans were owls. Mathematics and public affairs!)

'But the most important change of all is that I now see clearly the untenability of the hypotheses I maintained at the Jubilee of the Paradoxical. For the first time in my life I have a sense of settled conviction on such matters, a welcome substitute for the restless anxious feelings which I then strove to smother or to laugh out of existence. (*That's well.*) Consciousness is *no* mistake, and conscience is one of the most precious of our many endowments. I feel this so strongly that I am sorely tempted to rush into print at once on the subject for the benefit of my former associates. But I have learned the dangers of hasty generalisation, and my exposition of the *Relations between Religion and Science* I intend to be a thoroughly matured production. Pray forget, or think as charitably as you can of, my old follies (*No need to say that, though it is touchingly said*), and believe me, yours truly,

'Hermann Stoffkraft.'

[*'The little man is a trump, and we must get hold of him again. I am very curious to see his wonderful Countess, and to learn how such enormous changes took place in both in so short a time. Take care to have them at Elmsly House when I can manage to be there.*—E. H. 3/9/78.']

'Well,' said our host (after finishing his reading), 'I have now told you "what became of the Doctor," and I can but wish we could have him here once more. You well know the start which higher education has taken in this country, and the Doctor would be invaluable to us, either as a teacher or as an investigator.'

'And if he were to come,' said the Rev. Ralph Bemerton (evidently with an eye to possibilities), 'I think we could persuade him and the Countess to join the Church of England.'

'Cricket and lawn tennis for week-days,' said the irrepressible Frederick. 'I'll take the

Doctor in training, and Fanny shall have the Countess.'

'And to complete our catalogue of good intentions,' said the smiling host, 'I think I could induce the Doctor to become a regular member of the Paradoxical.'

www.ingramcontent.com/pod-product-compliance
Lightning Source LLC
Chambersburg PA
CBHW032223230426
43666CB00033B/881